Compositional Methods of Music Therapy

Nancy Jackson and Annie Heiderscheit

Compositional Methods of Music Therapy

Copyright © 2021 by Barcelona Publishers

All rights reserved. No part of this book may be reproduced, stored, or distributed under any circumstances, without prior written permission from Barcelona Publishers.

Print ISBN: 9781945411724
E-ISBN: 9781945411731

Barcelona Publishers
10231 Plano Rd.
Dallas TX 75238
Website: www.barcelonapublishers.com
SAN 298-6299

Cover design: © 2021 Matthew King

Dedications

I would like to thank my family, for their support and patience; my co-conspirator, Annie, for innumerable things both professional and personal; dear friends Susan Gardstrom and Jim Hiller, for stimulating deep thought about all things music therapy and for setting the bar high; and colleague Steve Sullivan for his invaluable assistance. I would like to dedicate this book to:

Ken
my beloved teacher, mentor, and professional dad

–Nancy A. Jackson, PhD, MT-BC

I would like to thank the clients and their families; of whose therapeutic journeys I have been privileged to be a part over my 30 years as a board-certified music therapist. It has been an honor to create and make music to foster and support their growth and healing. I am incredibly thankful to my husband, Jeff, and our children, Gray and Caroline, for their unending support for what I do in my professional life. I am grateful to my dear friend, colleague, and collaborator Dr. Nancy Jackson. I truly enjoy our process of co-creating, as we wrestle with how to present concepts until we find the solution. This book is also built on countless hours of brainstorming, discussion, and collaboration with dear friends and colleagues Dr. Susan Gardstrom and Dr. Jim Hiller. Thank you for the deep conversations that we have had as we have explored how to teach our students within a methods-based framework. I am also indebted to Steve Sullivan for sharing and contributing his expertise and creativity on this project. Last, my deep gratitude goes to Dr. Ken Bruscia for his mentoring, inspiration, and wisdom throughout the process of writing this book and beyond.

–Annie Heiderscheit, PhD, MT-BC, LMFT

About the Authors

Nancy Jackson, PhD, MT-BC, has been a practicing music therapy clinician since 1991, with experience in various mental health and medical settings as well as private practice. She earned her undergraduate degree in music therapy from the University of Wisconsin–Milwaukee and her graduate degrees in music therapy from Temple University. Her professional interests include anger and other emotions in music therapy; music therapy with chronic pain and illness; music therapy education and training; professional supervision and collaboration; and personal development of intercultural competence in support of DEI. She is a professor and director of music therapy in the Purdue University Fort Wayne School of Music, where she has taught since 2005. She lives in the Fort Wayne, Indiana, area with her husband, Mark; their sons, James and Nathan; and their dog, Lucy.

Annie Heiderscheit, PhD, MT-BC, LMFT, has been a practicing music therapy clinician since 1991, with experience in mental health, medical settings, addictions and eating disorder treatment, public schools, community-based settings, and private practice. She earned her undergraduate degrees in music therapy and music education from Wartburg College, completed graduate degrees from Iowa State University and the University of Minnesota, and has added graduate coursework at Temple University and Alfred Adler Graduate School. Her professional interests include music therapy with clients with eating disorders and substance use disorders, music-based listening interventions with critically ill patients, music therapy education and training, and collaborative and interprofessional practice and research. She is the director of music therapy and an associate professor at Augsburg University, where she has taught since 2013. She lives in the Minneapolis, Minnesota, area with her husband, Jeff; their two children, Gray and Caroline; and their little dog, Oliver.

About the Contributor

Steve Sullivan, MT-BC, currently works at Twin Cities Music Therapy Services and studied at Augsburg University. Before becoming a music therapist, Steve got his BA in music production from McNally Smith College of Music in St. Paul, Minnesota. He has worked for the past 27 years playing in bands, touring, recording, and teaching. He lives with his wife, Laura, and son, Jeffrey, and enjoys learning animation, playing video games, and helping others.

Table of Contents

PREFACE xi

CHAPTER 1: INTRODUCTION 3
Defining Compositional Methods and Method-variations 3
Orientations to Clinical Decision-Making 5
Levels of Structure 8
Culture, Cultural Identity, and Intersectionality 9
Trauma-Informed Practice 10
Technology 13
Dispositions of the Music Therapist 13
Terminology 17

CHAPTER 2: SONG TRANSFORMATION 25
Prerequisites 25
Risks and Contraindications 26
Affordances and Challenges 27
Orientations to Clinical Decision-Making 30
General Considerations and Procedural Guidelines 33
Special Considerations 40

CHAPTER 3: SONG TRANSFORMATION — CASE ILLUSTRATIONS AND EXAMPLES IN THE LITERATURE 43
Song Transformation with a Woman in
Residential Addictions Treatment 43
Literature Illustrating Song Transformation 47
Other Literature Related to Song Transformation 51

CHAPTER 4: SONGWRITING WITH INDIVIDUALS 57
Prerequisites 57
Risks and Contraindications 58
Affordances and Challenges 58
Orientations to Clinical Decision-Making 62
General Considerations and Procedural Guidelines 65
Special Considerations 72

CHAPTER 5: SONGWRITING WITH INDIVIDUALS—CASE ILLUSTRATIONS AND EXAMPLES IN THE LITERATURE 75
Songwriting with a Pediatric Intensive Care Patient 75
Literature Illustrating Songwriting with Individuals 80
Other Literature Related to Songwriting with Individuals 89

CHAPTER 6: SONGWRITING WITH GROUPS 99
Prerequisites 99
Risks and Contraindications 100
Affordances and Challenges 101
Orientations to Clinical Decision-Making 104
General Considerations and Procedural Guidelines 107
Special Considerations 116

CHAPTER 7: SONGWRITING WITH GROUPS—CASE ILLUSTRATIONS AND EXAMPLES IN THE LITERATURE 119
Group Songwriting with Adolescents in
Inpatient Mental Health Treatment 119
Literature Illustrating Songwriting with Groups 123
Other Literature Related to Songwriting with Groups 130

CHAPTER 8: INSTRUMENTAL COMPOSITION 137
Prerequisites 138
Risks and Contraindications 138
Affordances and Challenges 139
Orientations to Clinical Decision-Making 141
General Considerations and Procedural Guidelines 143
Special Considerations 150

CHAPTER 9: INSTRUMENTAL COMPOSITION—CASE ILLUSTRATIONS AND EXAMPLES IN THE LITERATURE 155
Composing with a Notational System for
Tone Chime Choir with Older Adults in Long-Term Care 155
Literature Illustrating Instrumental Composition 158
Other Literature Related to Instrumental Composition 159

CHAPTER 10: MUSIC COLLAGE 165
Prerequisites 166
Risks and Contraindications 166
Affordances and Challenges 167

Orientations to Clinical Decision-Making 170
Procedural Guidelines and Considerations 173
Special Considerations 184

CHAPTER 11: MUSIC COLLAGE—CASE ILLUSTRATIONS AND EXAMPLES IN THE LITERATURE 189
Music Collage with a Man with Developmental Disability 189
Literature Illustrating Music Collage 192
Other Literature Related to Music Collage 196

CHAPTER 12: USE OF TECHNOLOGY IN COMPOSITIONAL METHODS 201
Overview of Technology in Compositional
Method-variations 201
Clinical Technology Case Illustrations 203
Technology to Assist Client Engagement 208
Technology and Ethical Considerations 214
Considerations for Selecting Technology for
Your Music Therapy Practice 215
The Changing Nature of Technology 216
Review of Literature on Technology for
Composition Method-variations 217

INDEX 227

LIST OF TABLES
Table 1.0 Terminology 19
Table 2.0 Alteration Choices for Song Transformation 35
Table 3.0 Transformation Excerpt 46
Table 3.1 Guidelines for Music Therapy
Practice in Mental Health 53
Table 3.2 Guidelines for Music Therapy
Practice in Pediatric Care 54
Table 3.3 Guidelines for Music Therapy
Practice in Adult Medical Care 54
Table 3.4 Guidelines for Music Therapy
Practice in Developmental Health 54
Table 4.0 Song Composition Process 67
Table 5.0 Case Examples of Individual
Songwriting in the Literature 85

Table 7.0 Case Examples of Group
Songwriting in the Literature 128
Table 9.0 Case Examples of the Use of Instrumental
Compositional Method-variations in the Literature 160
Table 10.0 Considerations for Planning a
Music Collage Experience 176
Table 11.0 Guidelines for Music Therapy Practice
in Mental Health 197
Table 11.1 Guidelines for Music Therapy Practice
in Pediatric Care 198
Table 11.2 Guidelines for Music Therapy Practice
in Adult Medical Care 198
Table 12.0 Assistive and Adaptive Devices 210
Table 12.1 Case Examples in the Literature of the Use
of Technology with Composition Method-variations 219

LIST OF FIGURES

Figure 12.0 Illustration of Basic Signal Flow 202
Figure 12.1 Technology Illustration 204
Figure 12.2 Technology Illustration 205
Figure 12.3 Technology Illustration 206
Figure 12.4 Technology Illustration 208
Figure 12.5 Technology Illustration 212
Figure 12.6 Technology Illustration 212
Figure 12.7 Technology Illustration 213
Figure 12.8 Technology Illustration 214

PREFACE

This book on the selection, design, and implementation of compositional method-variations has had an interesting and extended evolution. It began as a joint venture by us and our dear colleagues, Dr. Susan Gardstrom and Dr. James Hiller. Our group felt stymied by the lack of appropriate textbooks for teaching undergraduate students about the methods and their variations and to help them develop critical thinking skills related to method-variation selection, design, and implementation for meaningful and effective music therapy treatment. So, we decided to create such a textbook and we worked toward that end for several years with the guidance of our mentor and publisher, Dr. Kenneth Bruscia. After lots of thinking and discussion and writing (and good food and wine), it became clear that covering all four methods in one book was a futile task—there is just too much information! In his wisdom, Dr. Bruscia asked for four separate texts, one for each of the methods and its variations. Thus, we set off on the road to the completion of this book, after having divided the methods volumes among the four of us and decided together on a shared general format for their layout.

We, the four of us, also worked together on articulating why we feel that a methods-based approach is necessary for the development of well-prepared, effective, and ethical music therapy professionals. We identified several reasons that we find this approach to be more useful than a populations-based approach and outlined them in a position paper that has been submitted for publication. As a philosophical premise for this book, we offer the following explanatory statements for the methods-based approach:

- A methods-based approach is respectful of each individual's personhood and recognizes that, though they might carry with them a diagnosis or be associated with a particular group with similar characteristics, they are a unique individual with their own strengths, talents, limitations, needs, values, and cultural matrix. They deserve to receive services that are responsive to who they are as a unique and valuable person.

- A methods-based approach, which allows for clinical decision-making in the moment, supports client agency in deciding what is best for themselves. Clinical decisions can be a collaborative effort between the client or group and the MT when they are not preplanned based on generalities.

- A methods-based approach to education allows the learning emphasis to be on our primary modality—music. It is reasonable to ask preservice MTs to learn about the intricacies of music and what it affords human beings. It is far less reasonable and, in reality, nearly impossible to ask them to learn the characteristics and intricacies of the many population groupings they are likely to encounter in clinical practice, *as well as* how to engage them in therapeutic applications of music. It is simply more effective and efficient to learn to address human needs with appropriate methods of music engagement.

- A methods-based approach leaves more room for reflexive practice. Because clinical decisions are made in relation to the needs of the client as they emerge and to what is happening in the present moment, it becomes a necessity to be mindful of self and other, to nurture the therapeutic relationship as the doorway to understanding and change, and to constantly evaluate the appropriateness and effectiveness of clinical music decisions.

- A methods-based approach welcomes alternate ways of thinking about the client, their needs, and the affordances of music because methods are not couched in a specific theoretical framework. Instead, the MT can shift their way of understanding the client, the client's needs, and the affordances of music to the schema that best fits the context and situation of the client, thereby allowing the most effective music therapy approach to take center stage.

- A methods-based approach may lead to better job satisfaction on the part of the MT. For the reasons already stated, a methods-based approach is likely to result in effectiveness demonstrated in treatment results for clients, which may translate to feelings of value and competence for the MT. Being free to respond flexibly to clients as their needs are presented in sessions combats monotony and boredom that can result from carrying out the same types of clinical applications day after day. Certainly, the MT who feels both effective and creative is more likely to be happy with their work and to consistently provide excellent service to their clients.

By emphasizing a methods-based approach, we are not dismissing the importance of understanding information-related diagnostic codes and population characteristics. Indeed, this information is highly important in terms of considering the types of structures that might be built into the implementation of any given method-variation with a particular client or client group, but it is not the basis for making clinical decisions about what music affords the client at any given moment in relation to their needs. Human beings have human problems that are unique to them, and, as MTs, we respond to client needs with the human experience of music that provides affordances that specifically answer their needs. Making clinical choices based on broad and general characteristics that describe an entire grouping of people cannot be called individualized treatment, nor can it be expected to be effective except on a chance basis. Using this information instead to inform the nuances of how we might design and structure a music experience can only increase its effectiveness.

In the chapters that follow, general procedural guidelines are provided for the selection, design, and implementation of compositional method-variations. Within the sections on planning, you will note that many questions are listed for your consideration.

These questions are meant to raise your awareness of specific knowledge about your client or group, which is where diagnostic and population information enters the picture. We do not attempt to outline these considerations for clients of every diagnostic or population grouping, as that would be impossible. As you increase your competency in understanding what music affords your clients, you will also better understand how to design those experiences so that your client can fully benefit from these affordances.

Chapter 1 introduces the four music therapy methods and the compositional method specifically. It prepares the student for developing the method-variations by discussing different orientations from which they might be applied and the role of structuring music experiences, as well as highlighting other considerations, including culture and intersectionality, trauma-informed practice, and the use of technology in the clinical setting. Personal dispositions of the MT related to methods-based thinking and practice are outlined and discussed. Finally, the terminology that will be used throughout the remainder of the text is presented, defined, and explained using a case example. We believe that learning and using this terminology from the beginning assists not only in communicating clearly with each other and with other professionals but also in developing the critical thinking that is required as students learn to approach music therapy clinical practice from a methods-based stance.in communicating clearly with each other and with other professionals but also in developing the critical thinking that is required as students learn to approach music therapy clinical practice from a methods-based stance.

The Introduction is followed by five chapters on the method-variations of composition alternated with five chapters of corresponding case examples and other literature for each method-variation. Chapters 2, 4, 6, 8, and 10 provide in-depth information for each method-variation, with general guidelines and considerations for selecting, designing, and implementing that variation. Special considerations related to the needs of different age groups are included. In our experience, case materials are of great assistance in students' understanding of clinical concepts and their applications, so Chapters 3, 5, 7, 9, and 11 each begin with an expanded case example of the specific method-variation. This is followed by other case examples in the music therapy literature that illustrate the MT's process of selecting, designing, and implementing the method-variation. These chapters also outline other literature that is related to the method-variation, such as research studies, clinical articles, and references to chapters in Barcelona Publishers' *Guidelines for the Practice of Music Therapy* series that include discussion of the method-variation. This final section of "other" literature is not comprehensive and doesn't include literature that focuses on the selection, design, and implementation process; it is instead intended to point the student in the direction of available resources should they choose to do further investigation into the method-variation, perhaps in preparation for a practicum placement or for other course assignments.

Finally, Chapter 12 provides discussion of and case examples related to the use of various technology to support compositional method-variations, including information and diagrams contributed by our colleague and tech wizard, Steven Sullivan, MT-BC. As music technology has grown exponentially in recent years, it is necessary for MTs to have some basic knowledge of what technology is available and how it can be used to support clients' compositional processes. The information in this chapter is elementary, but it is a good starting place for preservice MTs to begin incorporating technology resources into their method-variation preparation that will provide greatly expanded access to composition experiences for clients with all levels and types of abilities.

The book is designed in such a way as to be used either in whole from front to back or in parts in any order, based on the structure of the instructor's course. We have attempted to give sufficient illustrative material with the case examples to solidify students' understanding, as well as to connect them with other resources they can seek on their own in relation to other music therapy course work or because of their personal learning interests. As instructors ourselves, we value resources that are pragmatic and useful, and we have strived to present compositional method-variations in a pragmatic and useful way.

We also greatly value collaboration—working together. We see collaboration as the demonstration of the relationships that permeate music therapy, in the clinical setting with clients, in the classroom with students, and in professional life with our many brilliant, talented, and caring colleagues. So, it seems right that the road to completion of this text led us to a secluded cabin in central Wisconsin where the two of us worked together for the better part of a week—discussing, questioning, writing, erasing, sitting in silence, debating, and, of course, eating and drinking good food and wine—in a most joyous way. We sincerely hope that the result of our learning and working together makes a significant contribution to the learning and working together of others. We wish you joyful composing!

Compositional Methods
of Music Therapy

1

INTRODUCTION

Music therapists (MTs) can engage clients in therapeutic music processes in four different ways: re-creating, composing, improvising, and listening (Bruscia 2014). Within these four methods, there are infinite possibilities for the design and implementation of music experiences that are tailored to the specific needs and preferences of the client. This book focuses on the method of composition and developing an understanding of why and how you might design and implement variations of composition in music therapy sessions.

Composition is a music experience in which the MT assists the client or client group in creating their own new and unique music product. This might be a song, an instrumental piece, or some kind of multimedia music product, which can be re-created or listened to after its completion. An integral feature of this method is that the client is actively involved in the creation of the new music product; therefore, it should not be confused with instances in which the MT might compose a song or other music product for use in a music therapy session.

As MTs, we identify the strengths, limitations, and needs of our clients and make decisions about how engaging them in a music experience might help them to address an area of need, utilizing their strengths and in a manner that suits them in cultural and aesthetic ways. General categories of the many ways that compositional experiences can be designed are called *compositional method-variations*. These include *song transformation, songwriting, instrumental composition, music collage,* and *notational activities*. In song transformation, the client uses the structure of an existing song and changes it to make it unique to them, while in songwriting they compose a completely new song. Instrumental composition results in a piece of music with no words that can be re-created on one or more instruments. Music collage may utilize parts or all of songs and/or instrumental pieces, as well as sounds and other types of media, which are combined, arranged, or sequenced to create a new musical product. Notational activities involve the client creating a new notational system with which they compose a new piece or re-create a precomposed piece. The chapters that follow explore these compositional method-variations in more detail. Please note that notational activities are not included in a separate chapter because they are usually implemented as a part of other compositional method-variations, and there is no literature that addresses notational activities as a music experience in and of itself.

Selecting and designing appropriate and effective music experiences for our music therapy clients involves a critical thought process that includes consideration of multiple aspects of your client and their personal, interpersonal, and therapeutic contexts, as well as the nature of the various method-variations. A primary intent of this book is to help you to develop skills in recognizing and utilizing this multifaceted information to make clinical decisions that are meaningful, effective, and ethical, both in preplanning and during the music therapy session itself. This is a highly individualized process for each client and client group, so you will notice that the chapters that follow do not provide a how-to manual or "recipes" for what to do in sessions; instead, we hope the information herein will stimulate the development of your critical thinking and your creativity so that you select, design, and implement music experiences that are the most effective and most responsive to your clients' development and well-being.

You will learn about the different types of information regarding the client and the different means of observing and collecting this information in music therapy courses that address client assessment. Learning about and understanding the compositional method-variations and what each has to offer as a part of the therapeutic process is our concern here. This involves knowing what each method-variation affords the client, what types of demands it places on them, and how you can use these to build opportunities for the client to be challenged in ways that promote their growth and development relative to their identified treatment needs. Because the differences between method-variations and how they can be designed and implemented range from significant to highly nuanced, it is helpful to use terminology to describe these aspects of music experience so that they can best be understood as a part of our clinical thought process, as well as to support clear communication to others about why we are doing what we are doing with our clients within music therapy sessions. We have included nomenclature related to music therapy methods that will be used throughout this text in the Terminology section below. You are encouraged to learn this terminology, not just as a means to understand your clinical decision-making but also as a means to more effectively communicate with other MTs and professionals with whom you will work.

Orientations to Clinical Decision-Making

One of the advantages of learning to work from a methods-based perspective is that you are learning to work with our primary modality of music in a way that is applicable regardless of your personal theoretical orientation to therapy. This is also true about different perspectives on how to practice. In this book, we will consider the selection, design, and implementation of compositional experiences from both outcome and experience orientations to clinical practice. In these orientations, the roles of therapist and client may be different, as might the intentions and timing of design and implementation, but the compositional method-variations and their affordances and demands—and the resulting opportunities and challenges for the client—are consistent and drive the clinical decisions in both orientations.

Outcome orientation. The outcome orientation focuses on the needs of the client that have been identified through assessment and ongoing evaluation, for which the MT formulates specific goals and objectives. They then plan composition experiences specifically designed to move the client toward those objectives and implement them in the therapy sessions. In other words, this orientation is largely reflective of a cause-and-effect process. This is a problem-focused approach to treatment that is usually considered evidence-based because clinical decisions are supported by research or other practice-based evidence. It is an orientation that is common in many clinical settings that require clinicians to demonstrate the need for therapeutic services and to document client outcomes based on this work, such as settings that are funded through third-party payers (e.g., insurance companies, Medicare, waiver programs). In these cases, the MT may be expected to act in the role of "expert," maintaining coordination of the therapeutic process so that it can be objectively evaluated for efficacy.

An outcome orientation may also be adopted because of the nature of the client's problems identified for treatment. This may occur when the focus of treatment is less complex and easily quantified. For example, in a physical rehab setting when a client may be recovering from a time-limited injury or surgery from which full recovery is expected, a problem-focused, cause-effect treatment plan is a reasonable approach to assisting the client's efficient return to full functioning. Addressing additional domains of functioning, such as emotional functioning or social skills, may not be relevant in such cases.

The emphasis on planning for compositional experiences that are directly related to identified goals and objectives does not mean that you must carry out your plan at all costs. Indeed, the skilled MT practicing from this orientation will be carefully assessing the clients' responses to the music experience and their progress toward the treatment objectives during the session and making adaptations in the moment to the experiences in which they are engaged and to the plan in general in order to ensure consistent momentum toward those objectives. This flexibility within outcome-oriented practice is made possible by a thorough understanding of how to optimize the affordances and challenges inherent in the compositional music therapy method and its method-variations. Outcome-orientated thinking and practice will be addressed in each chapter as it applies to that compositional method-variation.

Experience orientation. The experience orientation to practice is focused on addressing a general concern that leads the client to therapy, but the treatment process emerges out of the client's engagement in the music process rather than being formulated as a cause-and-effect equation, and understanding of the client's needs and how to best address them is revealed through the various relationships in the music therapy process. Offering music as a process experience instead of crafting it to result in an outcome allows an unlimited amount of information about the client to be revealed, whether this is through patterns of expression and interaction, metaphor, or reflection of the inner life of the client. In this way, an experiential music process provides context and meaning to the client's behaviors and assists in clarifying a path toward wholeness and health around which the music experience is continually shaped. In other words, the MT brings to bear all available information about the client and their full understanding of the opportunities, challenges, and contraindications of the various method-variations in order to make clinical choices based on the client's response to musical interactions and what they reveal about the client's most pressing needs.

Typically, the kinds of treatment issues best addressed by an experience orientation to treatment are those of a more complex nature involving multiple domains of functioning or resulting from nonspecific or unidentified causes. As the MT and the client interact within music, both the MT's understanding of the client and the client's understanding of self come together as a process of problem-solving that is a collaborative effort; therefore, it is less likely that the MT will take on the role of expert. Likewise, the client can act as the expert on themselves and exercise agency in determining the course of therapy.

Session preparation is desirable for experience-oriented practice rather than session planning. Since there are no pre-identified objectives for treatment, it is not possible to effectively plan specific music experiences for the client. Instead, the MT needs to be prepared to respond to a variety of potential situations that might arise from the client's process. It is common for a music therapy model to be chosen as the structure for the session or a method-variation to be chosen as the starting point for exploration when working from an experience orientation. Session preparation helps the MT to have resources available as the client's process unfolds so that the music experience in the session can be shaped to support and encourage what emerges. For example, if the client is bringing in a song to share for song communication, the MT may want to be prepared with materials for song transformation or songwriting should the process move in that direction. Having instruments for both accompanying and improvisation would also be a reasonable choice to support a variety of musical exploration that might ensue from the song communication.

This highlights the importance of our full understanding of the affordances and challenges available to the client within any given compositional method-variation so that our choice of music experience for fostering exploration is one more likely to be effective in revealing the information that is needed for that therapeutic process. This understanding is also a necessity for determining how to transition from one method-variation to another as the client's needs emerge in the process. As you become more comfortable in thinking from a methods perspective and gain a firm grasp of the potentials of different method-variations, you will be able to make flexible and effective choices from moment to moment in response to the client's emergent needs. In the following chapters, experience-oriented thinking and practice will be addressed in relation to each specific compositional method-variation.

Levels of Structure

Selecting the better choice of method-variation to address the client's therapeutic problem at hand is not enough by itself to ensure that the music experience meets their needs. It is our responsibility as the MT to ensure that the manner in which the client is involved in the music experience is designed and implemented in such a way that they are capable of fully participating. This requires making decisions about the level of structure provided to aid the client in their participation. Structure can be provided verbally, musically, through modeling, by utilizing nonmusical resources, by providing for emotional safety, or by any combination of these. It is typical for us to adapt the type and amount of structure within music experiences multiple times throughout the session to maintain the client's engagement.

Structure is also the means by which we capitalize on the opportunities and challenges that we can provide the client within the music experience in order to keep them moving toward better health and functioning. For best effectiveness, it is imperative to build opportunities into the design of the method-variation so that the client can be challenged throughout the session without at any point being asked to do more than they are ready and able to do. Each method-variation can be designed with a wide range of structure, and most are amenable to changes in this structure while the client is actively participating in it, allowing us to shape the music experience to benefit the client as the experience progresses.

In music therapy, we are often asking our clients to take chances and to be vulnerable. Structure provides the means by which we can create a sense of safety for clients even as they are being challenged in ways that might feel uncomfortable. In order to do this, not only must we carefully prepare for how we will involve the client in the music experience but also we must exercise reflexivity within the session, observing the client's responsiveness, considering our own choices and manner of engaging the client, and adjusting these to simultaneously protect and push the client for optimum growth and development. Consider the affordances, challenges, opportunities, and demands of the compositional method-variations that follow and keep in mind the choices that are available to you for facilitating music experiences that balance opportunity and demand as well as safety and vulnerability.

As you adopt methods-based thinking and gain skill in working with the levels of structure available within the compositional method-variations that you use frequently with your clients, you may find that your effectiveness in providing for the needs of your clients takes a significant leap. As a result, you may feel more confident in music as a means for clients to utilize their full potential in their daily lives.

Culture, Cultural Identity, and Intersectionality

Culture encompasses many aspects that are a part of and influence our identity. Culture is informed by our beliefs, values, attitudes, social norms, and social and religious practices and is influenced by the environment, family, or community or an organization. Cultural identity is informed by our race and ethnicity, gender or gender identity, age, language, mental and physical abilities, socioeconomic class, religion, and sexual orientation. Intersectionality is the framework for understanding that each person has their own unique experiences and that the overlap of various social identities (race, ethnicity, gender, gender expression, appearance, sexuality, age, class, education, abilities, religious beliefs, political affiliation, etc.) may have contributed to a client's experience of discrimination and systematic oppression.

Understanding a client's culture, cultural identity, and intersectionalities is critical for us in developing a holistic awareness of the client and their experiences and in acknowledging that they may have experienced discrimination and oppression that have not been a part of our own experiences. In his ten considerations of man and music, Gaston (1968) indicates that our cultural matrix determines our mode of expression, recognizing that these intersectionalities are the essence of who a client is and have shaped and impacted their development. Understanding this informs the way in which we think about our client's needs and expands our acceptance of ways of self-expression beyond our own ways of expressing ourselves. Further, it informs our approach to the therapeutic process and our clinical decision-making.

Trauma-Informed Practice

A trauma-informed practice helps to address and answer many of the questions related to culture and intersectionality in the therapeutic process. Trauma-informed practice is a framework that acknowledges that any client seeking therapy may be a trauma survivor and recognizes that traumatic experiences can impact a client's emotional, physical, and spiritual well-being. Trauma-informed practice is *not* engaging the client in working through their trauma but is being aware of how to create a safe therapeutic environment for all clients. MTs engaged in a trauma-informed practice ground their work in these basic assumptions: (1) that they have a basic understanding of trauma and its wide-reaching impact, (2) that they can recognize the signs of trauma, (3) that they are able to integrate the six principles of trauma-informed care into their clinical practice, and (4) that they strive to avoid retraumatizing the client.

There are six principles that inform and guide trauma-informed practice that help to minimize the risk of re-traumatization and to improve the client's therapeutic outcome. These principles include safety, trust, and transparency; peer support; collaboration and mutuality; empowerment and choice; and cultural, historical, and gender issues. Safety encompasses both the client's physical and emotional safety, as well as protecting the client from internal or external threats. This includes creating a therapeutic space and environment in which the client feels safe physically and emotionally, as this will minimize the possibility of the client being triggered. We must also give careful consideration to the music being utilized in sessions as well as the musical elements (rhythm, tempo, dynamics, volume, dissonance, instrumentation, etc.), in order to avoid inadvertently triggering a client or causing harm. In the context of group sessions, we are responsible for ensuring the safety of all group members. This entails providing and reviewing group expectations to foster safety within the group. This also involves our management of issues that arise within the group that may threaten another client's sense of safety.

Trust is the foundation of healthy, helping relationships. Trust in a client–therapist relationship is established by developing and maintaining clear, reliable, and predictable boundaries. This helps to ensure that the client knows what to expect throughout their therapeutic process. Transparency is also a component of trusting relationships and entails being authentic, honest, and open with the client even when challenges may arise in the therapeutic work. Peer support is also a key element of trauma-informed practice, as being engaged with others who have a similar lived experience can offer a client an understanding that they are not alone in their experiences.

Collaboration and mutuality focus on embracing equality between the client and therapist in discussing and making decisions regarding the client's therapeutic process. It is important to understand the power differential inherent in the client–therapist relationship and recognize how this can impact the therapeutic work. This can help the therapist to recognize, validate, and value the client as an expert in their own therapeutic process. Respect for the client's knowledge and understanding of their own experiences fosters a collaborative therapeutic relationship.

Empowerment is a hallmark of trauma-informed practice, and it is supported by fostering the client's agency in making choices. Providing opportunities for choices within their therapeutic process enables clients to practice making informed, self-determined, and autonomous decisions and to take charge of their life within the context of therapy. As clients access and experience their own empowerment, they become capable and more confident in taking ownership of managing and living their lives as they integrate these skills outside the clinical setting.

Cultural, historical, gender, and identity issues are influential factors in the therapeutic process. Recognizing and understanding the client's cultural context and intersectionalities impacts whether a client feels valued and respected by the therapist and whether they can trust this relationship. It is important to understand that the families and ancestors of some clients have experienced emotional, psychological, and physical wounding across generations. Clients may have also experienced violence and trauma related to sexual orientation, gender identity, religious beliefs, disability, or economic class. Our acknowledgment of the presence and impact of historical trauma and trauma that has occurred related to identity is essential, as it will inform how we create a safe therapeutic relationship and environment for the client.

An aspect of historical trauma that is important to understand is cultural appropriation. For generations, dominant cultures have adopted elements or identities of minority cultures without permission. This act of integrating artifacts such as music and musical instruments from minority cultures without their consent with little or no concern for the meaning of these artifacts within that culture is appropriating them for our own use or gain. Music is a human experience that is influenced by culture; therefore, we need to understand the music the client prefers and its cultural implications and influences. To avoid cultural appropriation, we need to recognize the difference between using a tool or resource that is culturally appropriate for a client's therapeutic process and culturally appropriating these tools and resources. We can avoid cultural appropriation by being educated and informed about the music and instruments of a client's culture and deferring to the client's preference. As you make decisions about the compositional method-variations that you choose to implement with a client, the answers to a number of questions might prove helpful: What is the role of music in their culture? Does this music serve a specific purpose? What are the origins of this song? What is the significance of this song, its lyrics, and its accompaniment style? What instruments are unique to the client's culture? Are there cultural expectations about who plays the instrument and who provides the accompaniment? Would the client benefit from and are they interested in integrating this instrument into their compositional process?

Technology

Technology can be utilized and integrated into the composition process at different times and in different ways. The different types of technology, devices, and equipment that we use are dependent upon the needs and abilities of the client, the method-variation, instrumentation choices, and whether the client chooses to create a recording of their composition. Chapter 12 includes descriptions of various types of technology, as well as why and how they may be utilized to support the composition process. While this chapter does not provide step-by-step directions for how to use a device or software program, it does provide you with information to consider as you explore what technology may be most appropriate for use in different clinical settings. You will also find considerations regarding the use of technology and the implications this has on therapists and clients sharing recordings of compositions outside the clinical context and on social media platforms.

Dispositions of the Music Therapist

Thinking and working from a methods-based perspective requires some specific dispositions. While there are many skills that are necessary for clinical music therapy regardless of theoretical and practice orientations, such as developing strong functional music skills or communicating effectively in clinical documentation, methods-based clinical practice places personal demands on us that may not be as strongly emphasized in other ways of thinking and practicing. Dispositions should not be confused with having "the right personality" to be an MT. Instead, they are mind-sets and habits that are developed and practiced. Some dispositions may come naturally to us, while others may develop through maturation and still others may develop through education and training, supervision, and personal therapy. Luckily, learning to effectively design and implement compositional method-variations will help you to develop some of these ways of thinking about and interacting with your clients in the music therapy process. The dispositions that follow are by no means a definitive or exhaustive list of dispositions for music therapists but instead are those most relevant to clinical decision-making from a methods perspective.

Other-focus. It is logical that we must pay attention to our clients while engaging with them in music therapy experiences; however, maintaining focus on the client requires awareness and energy for a sustained period that is unlike our typical attention to others in daily interactions. Other-focus demands that we filter our internal thoughts and feelings, leaving aside those that are not directly related to the matter at hand in the session. For example, feelings of anxiety about an upcoming meeting with a supervisor need to be put aside, while an awareness of anxious feelings in relation to the client or the client's music may be important for informing clinical decisions and interactions. Other-focus involves attention to both self and other in that we are actively and judiciously filtering our own internal perceptions to include only those that are related to the therapeutic relationship and process. In making clinical decisions, other-focus leads us to make choices for the therapeutic benefit of the client and to reject choices that might be based on our preferences or what we had hoped or anticipated might occur during the session.

Deep listening. Like other-focus, deep listening is a multi-dimensional task demanding awareness and energy that is unlike most of the listening that we do in everyday life. In typical daily interactions, we may hear but not listen. In other words, we may take in information but not necessarily give that information careful consideration with regard to its deeper meaning and intent. Within the clinical process, we must not only listen to decipher meaning and intent but also expand our awareness so that we are listening with our ears, our eyes, and, in fact, our whole being. It is through this expanded multisensory awareness that we are able to "listen" to words that are spoken, to those that remain unspoken, and even to silences. We are able to "listen" to body language and to interpret affect and gestures that communicate emotional meaning. We are able to "listen to," interpret, and respond to the client's musical expressions and communications. Deep listening is predicated upon other-focus.

Seeking. Other-focus and deep listening alone are insufficient for our attempts to understand our client's experiences and what they might be attempting to express or communicate. We cannot directly know their thoughts and feelings; instead, we can interpret only what they present through the lens of our personal experience. Thus, we must be seekers. We must actively seek information to foster as accurate and complete an understanding of the client's experience as is humanly possible. Such seeking allows us to mitigate the tendency to misinterpret the client's personal and musical expressions and communications based on our own biases and preconceptions. As seekers, when we make clinical decisions about how to best support the client's therapeutic process through music engagement, this disposition assists us in being responsive in a way that truly respects and resonates with the client and that is most likely to be effective.

Seeking occurs before, during, and after each music therapy session. Beforehand, we collect information from various sources to inform our thoughts about the session. During the session, we may seek by verbally encouraging disclosure and clarification. Musically, seeking may occur through our elicitation of the client's expressions, elaborations, and musical interactions. We then seek verification, adjustment, or correction, which may be provided by the client through their verbal, gestural, or musical responses or any combination thereof. After the session, we reflect on what we learned; how it informs our way of thinking about the client, their music experience, and their overall therapeutic process; and what new questions have been raised. Finally, we recontextualize our new insights into our larger understanding of the client and then seek whatever is needed to move forward effectively.

In addition, we must also seek to broaden and deepen our own professional knowledge and skill, as well as to understand our role as a music therapist. In this way, music therapists must be lifelong learners. There is no end to what we can learn about music and music therapy, about our clients, and about ourselves. The more knowledge and skill we acquire, the more resources we have at our disposal to make clinical decisions that are sound, ethical, and helpful to our clients.

Discernment. Discernment involves discrimination, or the ability to distinguish differences. In the music therapy process, all participants, including the MT, will experience change on a continual basis. Yet, change alone does not necessarily indicate progress, so we must be able to recognize those moments of change that are therapeutically important. Discernment helps us to identify change that is significant and that informs and supports pertinent clinical decisions. It calls on us to understand what we are hearing, seeing, and experiencing in the client's moment-to-moment process and within the larger therapeutic context.

Flexibility. The unfolding nature of a music therapy session demands that we exercise flexibility to follow the process, change direction when indicated, and make moment-to-moment clinical decisions. While this could be construed as "just going with the flow" or doing whatever we feel like doing, this is not what is meant by flexibility. Flexibility is made possible by good preparation. Preparation includes collecting all available information about our clients, developing our own musical and therapeutic skills, considering and being prepared to provide the types and levels of structure that will allow clients' full engagement in the process, and focusing on and deeply listening to our clients during sessions to guide our decision-making. When we have properly prepared, we will have an internal repository of ideas, skills, and resources that can be called upon at any moment in the therapy process. When practicing from a methods perspective, it is the flexibility that allows us to make choices about how to engage the client through whatever method-variation is best suited to meet their health priority needs in the moment and as they are revealed throughout the process.

Courage. Allowing the above dispositions to positively impact our clinical practice means that we must be brave enough to accept that we are ultimately not in complete control of the music therapy process. We must trust that music, as a unique form of human experience, provides structures, challenges, and opportunities for clients to access and develop their healthiest selves. The courage that this trust requires is the same courage that helps us to be responsive to our client's needs as these needs emerge in musical and interpersonal interactions. The dispositions described above provide the foundation necessary to move ahead with courage, even as we recognize that human interactions cannot be predetermined or managed by a plan or a protocol. We must "be" in a manner that enables us to make clinical decisions throughout treatment that are relevant to our client, that call into play aspects of music and music experiences, and that propel the therapeutic enterprise forward, supporting the client as they access their own inner resources for healing and growth.

Terminology

There is a set of terminology utilized in this text that is important for you to understand. These terms establish a common nomenclature for communicating clearly about music therapy practice from a methods-based perspective. The following glossary and sample case illustration are intended to assist you in adopting this nomenclature.

Sample Case Illustration

Marcus is starting a music therapy group as a part of his new contract in an urban elementary school. The school has requested that he form a group to work on social skills for third graders in the special education program. The eight students who have been identified for this group include children with neurodevelopmental limitations such as Down syndrome and autism spectrum disorders. Marcus decides not to include a couple of students from the program in this group because they have pervasive developmental difficulties that severely limit their verbal and other interactive capabilities. He decides instead to work with those students individually in order to better meet their developmental and educational needs.

In order to assess the strengths and needs of the students in the group, Marcus chooses to involve them in a simple song transformation in which they have the opportunity to name and share with others some of their favorite things. He knows that he wants to identify specific behaviors that he can use to track the children's progress through the school year, but he also wants to allow the children to reveal things about themselves in the process of participating that will help him to better understand their needs. He selects a simple greeting song that he plans to teach the children as the ritual to start each of their sessions together. The song can easily have words changed in order for new options to be added. Marcus prepares the song by changing appropriate words to make space for the children's choices and creates a large number of magnetized pictures that can be placed on the board in the room to assist the children in understanding and remembering the new words they are adding to the song. He selects picture options related to favorite foods, favorite colors, and favorite animals. Marcus's original greeting song and its version prepared for song transformation are as follows:

Original:
My name is _____ and your friend I'd like to be.
There are lots of things we can share, you and me.
We're here together in music today.
We will have some fun as we sing and play.

Prepared for transformation:
My name is _____ and your friend I'd like to be.
I want to share with you something about me.
My name is _____ and here's a little fact,
My favorite _____ is _____.

  During the first session with the students, Marcus teaches them the original greeting song by rote. When students are comfortable in singing the original song with him, Marcus asks if they would be willing to help him get to know each of them better by sharing with him some things that they like. They agree, and Marcus explains how they will change the greeting song. The children choose colors as the first thing they want to share, and Marcus asks them to fill in the blanks of the song with their favorites. He pays attention to how well the children are able to take turns and provides some simple expectations for them to follow, such as raising their hands. He also lets them know what he will say to help someone to remember the expectations when they forget and interrupt others. Marcus makes mental notes of how easily the children become frustrated and how often he must provide verbal redirection. Marcus models remarks of encouragement and praise such as "Thanks for sharing that!" or "You did great waiting for your turn!"

In the next verse, when the students are asked to name their favorite animals, they have difficulty in identifying animal names, so Marcus places all of the animal pictures on the board to provide the students with visual cues as assistance. As students start naming their favorite animals, one student starts making sounds that match the animals. Marcus asks if the students would like to include appropriate sounds in their new song and quickly chooses a short harmonic progression to use as a bridge between verses so that students can add their animal sounds. The students moo and oink and bark and laugh with each other during each bridge.

When they have finally worked through the three new versions of the song and have sung them together with Marcus playing along on a ukulele, he talks to the children about what he has learned about them during the session and names a specific thing about each child. He asks the children to name things that they learned about each other. After talking about when they will meet again and about songs they would like to sing together, Marcus sings a good-bye song as the students return to their regular classroom with their teacher. Marcus makes notes about the strengths, limitations, and needs he identified for each student during their interactions and writes some group objectives for future sessions, including one about turn-taking behaviors and another about spontaneous social interactions.

Table 1.0
Terminology

Term	Definition	Clinical Illustration
Affordances	A specific interactive possibility that is naturally a part of the experience of music; different music experiences (therefore, different method-variations) will provide different sets of interactive possibilities for the person who is involved in this experience.	Song transformation affords participants means of expressing their own thoughts and feelings, and in a group setting specifically, allows students to cooperate and problem-solve together.
Opportunities	A set of circumstances or an allowance that facilitates the	Marcus structures the music experience to create the

	client's interactions within the affordances of a music experience; opportunities are created through choices that the music therapist makes in structuring and engaging the client in the music experience.	opportunity for individual students to access the affordance of self-expression while practicing some social skills, as well as providing the opportunity for a cooperative creative process to occur.
Challenge	An aspect of music experience that tests the limits of a client's capabilities in a particular area/domain in order to stimulate growth and development; the music therapist challenges the client by the way they structure the music experience in relation to the client's assessed need or their objectives for treatment.	Marcus asks students to name favorite things on their own and only provides assistance when they demonstrate that he has surpassed their current capability to act on their own.
Demand	A requirement of the music experience that the client must meet in order to fully and/or successfully participate.	The students must make choices to add their own preferences to the songs, utilizing both verbal and social skills.
Method-variation	A subcategory of a music therapy method that reflects specific ways of designing and implementing that method. Each of the four methods has many potential variations based on their design and implementation.	Marcus chooses the compositional method-variation of song transformation, which uses a precomposed song to structure the process of composition.
Prerequisite	A capacity, capability, or skill that a client must already possess in order to engage in a particular music experience.	The students need to have the capability to understand and participate in verbal interactions.

Risk	An aspect of a particular music experience that, under certain circumstances, can potentially be harmful or ineffective for the client.	Marcus watches for signs of frustration from the students, understanding that pushing past their capabilities may cause them to disengage from the experience.
Contra-indication	A combination of client characteristics or circumstances and the potential risks and demands of a particular music experience that have a high likelihood of leading to ineffective and/or harmful results for the client.	Marcus identified students who did not yet have the verbal and interactive capability to participate in the group because they would be unable to benefit from the affordances of the particular music experiences offered to this group.
Procedures	A series of actions taken to implement a method-variation.	Marcus taught the song, altered its structure, involved the students in rewriting it, performed it together with them, and reviewed what the group discovered.
Experience orientation	A manner of approaching a music therapy interaction that allows the therapeutic process to emerge naturally from the music engagement.	Marcus allows a spontaneous interaction from a student to suggest an addition to the structure of the song, acting on the student's agency to determine their own form of expression.
Outcome orientation	A manner of approaching a music therapy interaction with the intent of meeting pre-identified objectives.	Marcus wants to measure specific behaviors that he observes in the music session as a means of showing individual student progress over time.
Planning	The process of selecting and designing music experiences based on an understanding of the client's strengths and needs, with a focus on fostering therapeutic growth and	Marcus selects a simple song for students to help to orient them to the music session each week. The song also provides opportunities for students to verbally express their own ideas and learn about each other. He prepares materials

	development. students' full participation.	and resources to assist the
Engaging	Actively involving the client in responding to or making music and other interactions related to the music experience.	Marcus involves the students in singing the song, transforming it, and working cooperatively to create a personalized version of the song.
Observing	Intentional awareness of all salient aspects of the client's interaction with music, the environment, and all others involved in the music therapy session.	Marcus watches for indications of what the students can and cannot do as they participate and tests what types of assistance are successful in increasing their abilities in order to determine what he does next in the session, as well as how to plan for future sessions.
Adapting	Adjusting and modifying the music experience or other aspects related to the therapeutic process, in response to the client's identified and emergent needs, to ensure maximum therapeutic benefit.	The experience becomes too difficult for the students at one point, and Marcus responds by providing visual cues to assist them. When a student offers a spontaneous addition to the song, Marcus modifies the structure of the song to incorporate the student's addition.
Developing	Cultivating and expanding the music experience in order to explicate all of its affordances and capitalize on all available challenges relevant to the client's needs.	Marcus expands students' interaction with the music experience by incorporating a spontaneous response from one of the students into the structure of the new song.
Accompanying	Providing supportive musical interactions to highlight the client's creative expressions.	Marcus musically supports the song structure and the student's vocal expressions by providing a harmonic progression on the ukulele.
Reviewing	Processing through verbal, musical, or other creative means the content of the	Marcus talks with the students about what he learned about them and asks them to share

	music session and assisting the client's meaning-making and integration of the experience.	what they learned about each other.
Closing	Concluding the session in a manner that provides a sense of completion or a natural break in the process until the subsequent session.	Marcus and the students talk about when they will meet again and what they would like to do in that session.

In the chapters that follow, we will focus on each of the compositional music therapy method-variations and provide specific information about the prerequisites, risks, contra-indications, affordances, and challenges associated with them. We will look at each method-variation from both outcome-oriented and experience-oriented perspectives and will discuss general guidelines for selecting, designing, and implementing them. Each method-variation chapter is followed by a chapter that provides an original case illustration of that method-variation and a summary of other illustrations in the music therapy literature. We also provide a brief review of other literature related to that method-variation. These literature reviews are not comprehensive but give you direction if you are interested in looking more deeply into relevant research and case literature. Finally, we conclude the book with a chapter on technology and its use in compositional music therapy experiences.

References

Bruscia, K. (2014). *Defining music therapy* (3rd ed.). Barcelona Publishers.

Gaston, E. T. (1968). *Music in therapy.* Macmillan.

2
SONG TRANSFORMATION

A compositional method that offers great flexibility of application based on your clinical choices, song transformation makes use of the pre-existing structures of a song to engage the client in a creative process in which they can increase awareness of their behaviors, thoughts, and feelings and can express them within a new version of a song that is personalized. You assist the client in either replacing words or phrases in the original song with their own words and phrases while maintaining the melody or changing the melody and/or harmony of the original song while maintaining the original words. The result is an original song that borrows from a precomposed song but reflects the expressions of the client. It is a musical product that can be re-created or performed, recorded and replayed, or saved in a printed musical notation system. Clients may want to save their transformed song as a keepsake, as a record of therapeutic progress, as something to share with others, or as a gift for someone else.

Prerequisites

While some prerequisites for client participation in song transformation will be based on the level of structure that you choose to build into the experience, there are some general prerequisites that apply to most clients and client groups. Clients must have some receptive language capability and some ability to make their choices known. However, your understanding of the client's strengths and limitations and your subsequent preparation of resources can make song transformation accessible even to some of the most limited clients. For example, preverbal clients or those who have lost the ability to communicate verbally may be able to make choices by indicating "yes" or "no" to pictures provided by the music therapist or by using a device for assisted communication to express their wishes.

Risks and Contraindications

A number of risks may arise any time you ask a client to express themselves in a music experience. In song transformation, the content of the original song or the developing content of a transformed song may trigger difficult thoughts and feelings for the client. For example, original or new lyric content could bring up memories that trigger fear, anger, sadness or grief. Or, they could lead the client to experience cravings for substances or other addictive or ritualistic behaviors. Clients who have difficulty in problem-solving or making decisions might become frustrated with the completion of the transformation and give up or shut down emotionally.

In a group song transformation experience, lyric suggestions that involve negative behaviors or difficult feelings from one group member may encourage continued negative or dysfunctional responses and discussion from others in the group. If the group members cannot work cooperatively or manage differing opinions and ideas, arguments might ensue that will disrupt the transformation process. Or, one or more members of the group may feel that their ideas or offerings are not heard, valued, or accepted by the group. Likewise, the group may make final decisions for the transformed song that result in one or more group members feeling as though the final product does not represent them.

Most of these risks can be reasonably minimized by your careful planning. Understanding the appropriate level of structure needed by a client or client group, as well as their strengths and limitations, will assist you in structuring the song transformation experience to avoid obvious risks. Awareness of the potential risks of song transformation for any particular client or group will allow you to recognize difficulties that unexpectedly arise and to act quickly to minimize disruption to the experience or danger to the client or to group members.

Song transformation experiences are contraindicated for those in minimally conscious states, those who do not have language skills, and those who are unable to make their wishes known to others. Song transformation may also be contraindicated for those in a psychotic state in which they are so disoriented to reality that they cannot make use of language in a meaningful way or who cannot grasp the abstract ideas of melody and harmony. In these cases, it is better to wait until some cognitive stability is achieved prior to attempting song transformation. Likewise, some individuals in advanced stages of dementia may be too disoriented to effectively use language or work through a process in order to complete a song transformation.

Affordances and Challenges

There are a number of affordances inherent in the song transformation process and a number of challenges that you might choose to highlight in order to address the needs or treatment objectives of the client. Your choice of song transformation and of a particular manner of structuring a song transformation experience is based on the needs of the client, the strengths that the client brings into the session, their musical preferences, and the strength of the therapeutic relationship between you and the client. The following are common affordances and challenges that may be utilized as the basis for clinical decision-making when employing song transformation. They certainly are not all-inclusive, and the more creatively you think about the needs, strengths, preferences, and comfort level of the client, the more you may discover other affordances and other challenges to stimulate the client's growth and development within song transformation. Whether you are working from an outcome-oriented perspective or an experience-oriented one will have an impact on the affordances and challenges inherent in the experience, as will the individual or group format of the session and the age of the client.

Decision-making. In song transformation, the client must make decisions about changing the original song in order to personalize it. This might involve replacing words, phrases, complete lines of lyric, or even the entirety of lyrics for a song. Likewise, it might involve changing the tonality of the song, the harmonic progression, or the melody in order to provide a different mood or meaning for the original lyrics. Even the rhythmic structure of a song can be changed, resulting in a song with a significantly different expressive feel. No matter how much or how little of the original song is changed, transformation of the song will require that the client make choices about those changes. The challenge of decision-making may be the primary reason for engaging the client in song transformation, or it may be that decision-making may present the opportunity to address other issues relative to the client's needs, such as increasing self-awareness or working through feelings and emotions related to the topic of the song.

Self-organization. The original structure of the song being transformed affords the client a chance to organize their own behaviors, thoughts, and feelings. This might take the form of providing replacement words that fit the song topic or arranging rewritten words or phrases in an order that makes sense. It might challenge the client to attend to the task at hand long enough to complete the transformation in a meaningful way. For the transformed song to have meaning or therapeutic value, the client must be able to recognize themselves in the transformed song, which demands that they meet the challenge of organizing their participation in the transformation.

Problem-solving. Any type of creative activity is a process of problem-solving. Numerous problem-solving affordances are inherent in a song transformation. This may occur in a concrete way as the client works with the words they have chosen to make them fit into the rhythmic structure of the precomposed melody. It might be a more abstract type of process as the client searches for the most accurate words to express their feelings or as they consider various choices for answers to a question that the song poses. Problem-solving may be a treatment focus for a client, in which case you might select a song transformation experience because it challenges the client to problem-solve. Or, because problem-solving is an affordance of song transformation, a client might work through various scenarios for responding to a given situation through transformation of verses of a song.

Self-expression. Regardless of the level of structure you build into a song transformation experience, the client will be engaged in making choices that reflect their own wishes, thoughts, ideas, and feelings, making self-expression a primary affordance of this method-variation. On a basic level, this might be indicating yes or no to choices for a client who cannot verbally express themselves. On a concrete level it might be selecting likes and dislikes or feelings and emotions in order to complete lines of lyric. On an abstract level, this might be describing personal experiences, thoughts, and feelings in creative or metaphorical lines of lyric or reflecting them in rhythmic or harmonic changes to the song's structure.

Thematic exploration. Song transformation allows focus on a topic related to the client's goals and objectives for treatment and affords a means of working through the issues around this topic. For some clients, this may take the form of identifying feelings and emotions related to the topic. For others, problem-solving might occur around exploration of reactions, responses, and behavioral patterns. The structure of the original song, when carefully chosen for appropriateness to the task at hand, can provide some ease in this exploration while retaining just enough challenge to keep the client considering new choices and making personal meaning within their transformed song.

Cooperation and conflict resolution. In a group format, the song transformation process affords the group members means of working together and often requires them to work through disagreements or differences in opinion. It also requires them to listen to one another and to practice social skills such as turn-taking. You may plan and apply the necessary structure for the experience to make cooperation possible for the group. Or the group may work together to formulate rules for their process of completing a song transformation.

Orientations to Clinical Decision-Making

Outcome Orientation

If you are working from an outcome orientation, you will be thinking about how the completion of the song transformation will assist the client in meeting specific treatment objectives based on pre-identified needs. These needs are those that you have identified through your music therapy assessment. Perhaps the client needs to be more assertive in making choices, or maybe they need to learn and remember steps for the completion of a task, or maybe a group of clients needs to practice the social skills of taking turns and tolerating differing opinions. Song transformations offer multiple affordances for demonstration of behavioral, cognitive, and social growth and development. In an outcome-oriented approach, song transformation will lend itself to defined and measurable results. The role of the music and the various relationships within the music experience is to address the problem and to affect change toward the objective in a cause-effect manner.

Music as agent. In a song transformation experience, the client and therapist may be using the original song structure as a means of imparting information about completion of tasks or about behavioral responses. For example, in transforming a song with new lyrics about appropriate behavioral choices that can be made at times when one is feeling angry, the client mentally rehearses these choices every time the new song is sung. Thus, the music becomes the agent for behavioral change as the client can more easily recall alternative behavioral responses when feeling angry.

Music as skill. When song transformation is chosen for the purpose of encouraging and practicing skills, these skills are addressed by the actual process of the transformation. In other words, the activity of transforming the song automatically requires the skills that are being targeted for development. Additionally, the skills that are developed through the song transformation process should be generalizable to other situations outside of music. As an example, perhaps a client needs to develop skills in interactive listening and turn-taking. In a group song transformation experience, that client will need to listen to the ideas of others, formulate appropriate content to add to the song content, allow others to make suggestions and express their preferences, and work cooperatively to complete the song transformation. In assisting the client to listen to other's expressions, waiting for his turn to add meaningful content to the group song, and working cooperatively to decide the final version of the transformation, you will be providing an opportunity for the client to demonstrate his progress in meeting the treatment objectives. Then, in other situations in which listening and turn-taking are required, the client will be better prepared to utilize those skills.

Music therapy protocols. Song transformations can be structured in such a way as to provide the vehicle for a treatment protocol that has been defined based on the client's assessment and outlines specific objectives that are to be achieved over the course of time. For example, a client may be working on a general goal of improving problem-solving skills. Objectives for the client are arranged in a developmental order: (1) make simple decisions, (2) identify two or more options and make a choice, and (3) identify options related to a problem and select the better choice. Implemented within a song transformation experience, the directives for the client might be first to replace one word in each phrase of the song's refrain, then to create a verse addressing the refrain by brainstorming several ideas and selecting one on which to focus the verse. This process might be repeated two or three times to create multiple verses. Finally, a verse can be created that sums up the meaning of all of the other verses by exploring what the transformed song now expresses. The progression through different levels of decision-making that occur over multiple iterations of the song transformation process provide the music therapist with multiple points of measurement to determine if the objectives of the protocol are being met.

Experience Orientation

If you are working from an experience-oriented approach, a song transformation allows the client to experience their own thoughts, feelings, and behaviors as they become manifest in new lyrics for the song or are represented by the sounds of changed melody lines and harmonies. A song transformation experience from this orientation is chosen relative to the client's need in therapy but does not have pre-established objectives (e.g., take turns, or identity feelings). Instead, the immediate needs of the client are revealed in the process of song transformation, and you will assist them in clarifying, exploring, or working through the therapeutic material as you complete the transformation.

Music as process. A song transformation experience may grow out of a discussion or out of some other type of music engagement with the client as a particular therapeutic need emerges that can be effectively addressed by the affordances of a compositional process. For example, while listening to a particular song that the client has chosen, the client talks about how the song makes them wish for something in their own life. The music therapist may engage the client in a discussion about these wishes and then use the song chosen for listening as the structure to express the client's wishes by replacing words and phrases of the lyrics with the client's own thoughts. As the client identifies ways to change words within the original song, they may also express feelings related to those wishes that prompt a deeper discussion of the topic and perhaps further alteration to the original song in terms of words or harmonic or rhythmic structures. In the process of completing the song transformation, the client may have identified ways to make specific changes in their life in order to address something they feel is lacking.

Music as representation. When song transformation is used as a means of representation, the resulting song product is evidence of what occurred in the client's therapeutic process. As an illustration of this, a music therapist might suggest a song transformation experience to a group that is approaching termination at the conclusion of a treatment program as a way to review their progress. The group uses a song that they have sung frequently as a part of their therapeutic process in music therapy. They work together to replace the words of the song with their thoughts and feelings about what they have learned and their wishes for themselves and each other as they prepare to move on. As they start to select ideas for lyrics, the group decides they want to include something specific about how each group member has grown while in treatment. When the transformation is complete, the music therapist assists them in recording a group performance of the song, a copy of which is provided to each group member as a record of their work together.

General Considerations and Procedural Guidelines

Once you have decided that a song transformation experience is a good choice to meet your client's needs and treatment objectives, you will plan, implement, observe, and evaluate your choice for its appropriateness and effectiveness. The following steps are general guidelines and procedures that apply to most song transformation experiences. They are certainly not all-inclusive, however, and you are likely to develop your own creative ideas as you gain experience in facilitating song transformations.

Planning

- Determine your client's specific abilities and limitations in relation to participating in a song transformation experience, including all of the relevant domains of functioning.

    - Verbal or nonverbal?
    - Concrete or abstract thinking?
    - Reading and writing capability?
    - Able to attend, and for how long?
    - Able to identify feelings?
    - Able to express feelings?
    - Able to work with others?
    - Musical preferences?
    - Musical experience?
    - Musical knowledge?

- Based on your client's abilities and limitations, decide on a level of structure that you will provide to ensure that your client can fully engage in the transformation experience.

    - Will they need pictures or a word list in order to provide lyric replacement?

- Can they effectively select and replace single words, phrases, whole lines, or all of the lyrics of a song?
- Can they identify sounds that convey moods or meanings?
- Can they work independently and write down their ideas?
- Can they read to perform the final product, or do they need pictures or other cues to assist them?

- Select a song that matches the client's musical preferences, matches the desired content of the intended focus of the experience in some way, and lends itself to transformation. It should be known by the client or very easily learned in order to assist the transformation process. It should also lend itself well to the removal of words or changes to musical aspects relevant to the client's abilities (e.g., removal of one word, removal of full lines of lyric, easily changed harmonic structure). It might be that you can work with your client to pick an appropriate song for transformation if their abilities allow it, or they may be able to suggest an appropriate song on their own.

- Prepare the song and other necessary resources for the session. Along with knowing the song well yourself and having a musically pleasing accompaniment ready, you will also prepare the resources that will facilitate your client's full participation, which might include but isn't limited to the following:
  - Lyric sheets with blanks or paper and pens or pencils
  - A smart board, or a white board or flipchart and markers
  - Pictures or word cards and a magnetic or cork board
  - A word list of feelings and emotions, actions, objects, or other appropriate suggestions for word substitution
  - A list of sample harmonic progressions in different tonalities

Engaging

- Describe the experience to the client, including the purpose and what the client will be asked to do.

- Play and sing the original song with the client. Point out the places where the client will replace original lyrics with their own words or discuss this with the client to make these choices. Or, assist the client in identifying how to make the song sound differently by altering other musical aspects such as melody, harmony, or rhythmic structures.

- Introduce the resources that will be used for the experience (e.g., lyric sheets with blanks for new words, pictures that clients will select, or harmonic progressions in varying meters).

- Provide the least amount of needed assistance for the client to select or develop new words or melodic/harmonic aspects for the song.

- At the completion of the transformation, sing the new song together and, if appropriate, make a recording of the performance. For clients with reading capability, copies of newly transformed lyrics can be provided to document the work done in the session.

The following gives simplified examples of implementing song transformation based on lyric replacement and based on alteration of musical elements. Again, this is not a recipe for how to do a song transformation but instead is one way of organizing the process. Of course, given the needs and the capabilities of the client, these approaches to transforming a song can be combined or can be alternated as a means of creating multiple iterations within a process. Table 2.0 illustrates different ways to approach and structure the song transformation experience.

Table 2.0
Alteration Choices for Song Transformation

Alteration of Lyrics	Alteration of Music Elements
Identify words, phrases, or sections of lyric that are appropriate for replacement.	Identify the musical elements that when changed will best result in a transformed expressive quality.
Prepare lyric sheets or a white board/ flip chart so that it is clear where	Prepare choices or examples of changes to assist clients, such as a list

personalized choices can be added.	of chord progressions or rhythmic/meter options.
Discuss the intent of the experience with the client and brainstorm some ideas around the topic at hand.	Discuss the intent of the experience with the client and brainstorm some ideas around the topic at hand.
Using ideas from brainstorming and reasonable amounts of the original song (e.g., one stanza or one verse), assist the client in beginning to fill in blanks with lyrics that express their thoughts and feelings.	Using ideas from brainstorming and reasonable amounts of the original song (e.g., one stanza or one verse), assist the client in trying out different musical changes and selecting those that reflect what they want to express.
Consider the whole of the section and verify that the client is happy with it or help them to make adjustments as necessary before moving on to the next section.	Listen to the whole of the section and verify that the client is happy with it or help them to make adjustments as necessary before moving on to the next section.
When all sections are finished, review the whole song and determine if it is ready, if words or phrases to be adjusted, or if it would benefit from adding more sections.	When all sections are finished, review the whole song and determine if it is ready, if any of the musical changes need to be adjusted, or if it would benefit from adding changes to additional musical elements.

When the client is satisfied that the product reflects what they had intended to express, perform the song as a complete whole. Do this together with the client if possible or, if they have the musical skill to do so, encourage them to perform their transformed song themselves.

Discuss the client's reaction to their transformed song and help them to identify insights that they may have gained about themselves and their therapeutic process.

Help the client to decide the final format of the song product and about what they will do with it. If the client can participate in creating the final format or can actually do it themselves, assist them in that completion process. Otherwise, make the final product and present it to the client.

Observing

- Pay attention to the amount of effort the client is putting into the experience and adjust your assistance as needed.

- Is the client making thoughtful choices or just filling in the blanks in a random way?
- Might discussion help to make the client's choices more meaningful?
- Would increasing or decreasing the number of choices help?

- Notice how the client problem-solves during the experience and make note of where they demonstrate difficulty or frustration.

  - Is there difficulty or frustration with the completion of the song, the topic of the song, or the feelings the song or the process elicits?

- Make note of the client's reactions to the transformed song.

  - Does the client seem proud of or happy with their choices?
  - Does it seem to elicit an emotional response from the client?
  - Does their response indicate that more needs to be added to the song to make it complete or to reach a particular insight?

Adapting

- Consider the extent and quality of your client's participation. Is the client having difficulty in fully engaging in the transformation process? If so, why is this? How can you change the structure of the experience to increase their active engagement?

  - Have they lost interest because it is too easy or too hard?
  - Do they understand what they are being asked to do and why?

- Consider how the experience is unfolding. Is the experience effectively addressing the concern it was meant to address? Sometimes active engagement does not lead toward the desired outcome, and alterations must be made to the directives or to the structure of the experience.

- Might giving specific choices help movement toward the objective?
    - Can a different perspective be offered on the process? (You've identified lots of feelings to include. Now, can you identify some actions in response to these feelings?)

- Is a more urgent need emerging as the client participates in the experience?

    - Has the transformation process brought up new feelings or new insights that might change the topic of the transformation?
    - Should the transformation experience be transitioned into another method-variation in order to better address the issue at hand?

Is the client meeting the challenges built into the experience too easily? If so, should the directives be changed to create more challenges to improve skill or to move the client deeper into their therapeutic process?

Developing

- Has the client fully realized the affordances of the transformation process, or might they benefit from some elaboration?

    - If the transformation is completed quickly, what more can be done with it? Consider adding more verses or working with more focus on an aspect not yet addressed.
    - If there is another song that would be a good fit with the first song used, can you create another transformation focusing on another aspect of the topic being explored?

- Can secondary needs or treatment objectives also be enfolded into the transformation process? For example, if the client is successfully expressing feelings, can they also start to explore and incorporate ideas for coping skills related to these feelings into the transformed song?

Accompanying

- Work on incorporating stylistic elements into your accompaniment that reflect the content of the client's transformation. This might include selection of an accompaniment instrument that the client prefers, an accompaniment pattern or musical style that reflects the client's culture, or a stylistic accompaniment that emphasizes the mood of what is being expressed.

- When feasible, give the client agency to accompany themselves and provide what is needed musically to make the client's own music-making pleasing to them.

- While it is your job to ensure that the final product is musically and expressively satisfying to the client, always keep in mind that it is the client's or the group's expressions in the transformed song that need to take center stage. In other words, providing a beautiful accompaniment that distracts from what the client has created will not allow the affordances of the method-variation to be fully realized. Balance your accompanying capabilities with the needs of the client and the intended expression of the new song, like a frame enhances and brings focus to a picture.

Reviewing

- Once the song has been transformed, perform it with the client. Let the client talk about how they feel about it and whether they are pleased with the product. Return to working on it if the client doesn't feel it is just right.

- Review the intent of the experience and help the client to determine if the product has met that intent.

- Discuss what comes next if the transformed song is part of an ongoing therapeutic process. Can the song be used as a springboard into another type of musical exploration? For example, if the client has gained an insight as a result of the transformation process, perhaps that insight might be explored through improvisation or through some song communication.

- Decide the final format of the product.

    - Should it be recorded, transcribed into musical notation, and so on.
    - What should be done with it? Does the client want to gift it to someone? Share it with the treatment team or another therapist? Keep it as part of a journal or a record of progress in therapy?

Closing

- If the transformation is not yet complete, help the group to summarize where they are in the process and how they will continue in the next session.

- In most cases, performing the song together a last time can help to make the session feel complete even if the song has not been completed.

Special Considerations

With children. Generally speaking, children have not developed the ability for abstract thought, and this will affect your planning for a song transformation. Pick songs that are easily and concretely understood and that have clear options for word or phrase replacement. Musical elements can be transformed if presented with concrete descriptors such as fast/slow, loud/soft, happy/sad. Keep in mind as well that children's singing range is often still limited, so choose songs that have melodies within the range of one octave at most and which largely move in a stepwise direction with only small interval leaps. Reading and writing skills may also be limited or undeveloped in children. Be prepared with plenty of visual aids to assist in the transformation process.

With adolescents. Safety is a special concern for adolescents who are typically struggling with identity formation and may be especially sensitive to perceptions of rejection or judgment by their peers. Remember that this sensitivity may be increased by the intersectionality of numerous cultural aspects, such as race, religion, socioeconomic status, and gender identification and expression. Even differences in music preference can set the stage for exclusion or ridicule. The establishment of firm group rules related to the process of song transformation is necessary to protect teenage group members' sense of safety in sharing thoughts and feelings. Allowing the group members to play a significant role in determining the rules can help to hold them accountable for their behavior while working together. Modeling is also important for demonstrating to group members that everyone's thoughts and opinions are welcomed and valued. Don't move ahead through the steps of the song transformation without stopping to check in with everyone to confirm that they are feeling a part in what is being created.

With older adults. Older adults may experience sensory deficits and other physical problems that are not directly related to their reasons for being in treatment, such as declines in hearing and sight and decreased ability for fine and gross motor movement. Be sure to assess these physical and sensory capabilities in preparation for any song transformation experience because they may have a significant impact on the resources that you provide as a part of the process. While your older adult clients may have excellent command of language, they might have difficulty in reading or writing. Consider whether large-print lyric sheets are warranted or whether you should forgo those in favor of writing on a board in large, bold-color print. Consider the arrangement of the clients in the treatment space and ensure that each has a direct line of sight and that those with hearing deficits are closest to the front. Most older adults lose some hearing in higher registers as they age. Choose songs that do not have an excessively large melodic range and perform them in lower keys to accommodate the hearing and vocal capabilities of your older clients.

Conclusion

The song transformation experience provides plenty of flexible structure that you can maximize to assist clients and client groups in actively participating in a compositional process regardless of most limitations. Your understanding of the affordances of this method-variation and of how to shape opportunities and manage the amount of challenge in the experience will determine the extent to which it effectively answers the clients' needs. Proper preparation for implementing the song transformation, including gathering and preparing needed resources, thinking through potential responses from clients, and considering any difficulties that might arise, will help you to make clinical decisions in the moment that are respectful and responsive to your clients and lead to a meaningful experience. Proper musical preparation will allow you to focus on supporting and focusing the therapeutic process while creating an aesthetic musical stage on which to highlight the clients' therapeutic content. Finally, as you become comfortable with facilitating the client's therapeutic process through song transformation, you will begin to recognize appropriate points within the experience at which you may consider transitioning into another method-variation to continue moving the process forward.

3

SONG TRANSFORMATION — ILLUSTRATIONS AND EXAMPLES IN THE LITERATURE

Song Transformation with a Woman in Residential Addictions Treatment

Dee was a 46-year-old who had been sentenced to court-ordered addictions treatment at a residential facility for women. Because of her long history of alcohol and opioid use, she had been in and out of treatment multiple times, had lost custody of her children, and had had a string of unhealthy, unsuccessful, and sometimes violent relationships. When she began working with the MT in weekly individual sessions, she was feeling hopeless and was grieving the many losses she had sustained through her life, many due to drug- and alcohol-related behaviors. She felt that if she could not find a different way forward during this round of treatment, she was unlikely to survive after she left.

The MT first started working with Dee in group sessions at the facility but observed that Dee never had enough time in a group format to really identify and express her feelings about what seemed to be a bottomless pit of losses. Dee was happy to begin individual sessions and told the MT that she felt desperate to "get stuff out." The MT initially began by involving Dee in improvisation to give her some nonverbal freedom of expression. After a couple of sessions, however, it became clear that Dee would easily become stuck in her emotions. The MT assessed that while Dee's emotions were difficult ones—grief, anger, sadness—she also felt safe and "at home" in these feelings and wasn't motivated to explore other ways of being because of fear of the unknown.

Dee's favorite style of music was country and western, and the MT knew several different songs in this style that were positive and hopeful. She thought that song transformation using a song that Dee might know and like would afford her a safe structure in which to problem-solve and "test out" different ways to feel, act, and think about her experience in life. She made a list of songs that would work well for song transformation and had lyrics sheets ready for each of the songs. She described the song transformation process to Dee, who liked the idea of doing something creative to figure out some answers in her life. Dee chose "I Hope You Dance" by Lee Ann Womack from the list of songs the MT provided as one she especially liked.

This song was one that the MT had included because she could build opportunities into the song transformation process for challenges that could be graduated in difficulty, allowing the demands on Dee to be gentle to start and become more direct and confrontational as she worked through her issues. To begin the process, the MT asked Dee to listen to the song while looking at the printed lyrics and to mark phrases in the song that she thought were like her by underlining them. Dee was then asked to change the pronouns from "you" to "I" in these places in the lyrics so that the song could begin to relate specifically to her. In looking at what she identified, Dee was able to see that she had only identified things that sounded bad or wrong to her as things that were like her.

The MT gave Dee a clean lyric sheet, and they listened to the song again. This time, Dee was asked to mark the phrases in the song that she wished were like her. When asked to change the pronouns in those phrases to make them pertain to her, Dee said that she was trying hard to be honest with herself, so she did not want to say something that simply wasn't true. With encouragement from the MT for Dee to look more closely for something that she could honestly say about herself, Dee was able to change the refrain from "I hope you dance" to "I wish I could dance." At the end of the session, the MT and Dee discussed the fact that she could not see herself being different at this point in time and that perhaps she could start by identifying what she didn't want to do and feel anymore.

In the next session, the MT asked Dee to make a list of all of the things that she wished she hadn't done, as well as what she hoped she would not do in the future. While this seemed to be a negative approach to take, the MT recognized that by specifically identifying these things, Dee was naming the problems that she needed to tackle in order to problem-solve a different way to live. Dee was able to name a long list of things that she didn't want. Then, returning to the song, the MT asked Dee to identify one verse that she wanted to rewrite using thoughts from her list. With some assistance from the MT in arranging words so that they fit the original melody rhythmically, Dee wrote the following verse:

I wish I didn't fear what people think about me
I wish I didn't always not change
I want to stop taking bad chances and take good ones
I want to stop pushing my kids away
I wish my life didn't make me angry
I wish I could accept things and move on
I wish I would let myself hope for something good
I want to make better choices for myself

I wish I could change
I wish I could dance

The MT and Dee sang the rewritten verse together with the MT providing piano accompaniment, and Dee stated that it felt good to say these things about herself out loud. The MT encouraged Dee to share her verse in her other therapies. Dee reported in her next session that she had chosen to share her verse in her community-based Narcotics Anonymous meeting and had received lots of helpful feedback from others there. The MT noted that Dee's affect was brighter and that she seemed to be fortified by having others respond in a positive way to her song. The MT felt as though she could increase the challenge in the transformation process and suggested that Dee find one thing in her rewritten verse that she felt she might be able to change in the future. Dee chose the line "I want to make better choices for myself," and she and the MT went back to brainstorming ideas for how Dee might make better choices.

In the next three sessions, which led up to Dee's impending discharge from the program, the MT continued increasing the amount of problem-solving that she encouraged Dee to do, using both the original song and the sections that Dee had already transformed as a springboard for moving the process forward. In their last session together, they reviewed the original song and the various versions that Dee had transformed. The MT helped her to verbalize what had changed for her at each iteration of her new song so that Dee had a sense of how her thinking was changing over time. Dee decided that she had one more change to make and asked for the refrain to be "I am really changing. I am going to dance." Dee asked if the MT would make a recording of the song for her so that she could remind herself of what she wanted for her future. Dee did not want to hear herself sing because it made her uncomfortable, so the MT both sang and accompanied on piano to make the recording. On the day Dee left the program, the MT presented her with a finalized copy of the transformed song in print and sent an audio file to Dee's cell phone so that she could access it there whenever she wanted to remind herself of her own wishes and hopes and of her progress in music therapy.

Table 3.0
Transformation Excerpt

Original Lyrics (excerpt)	**Finalized Song Transformation (excerpt)**
I hope you never fear those mountains in the distance, Never settle for the path of least resistance,	I am focusing just on what I think about me So I can keep changing and growing.
Livin' might mean takin' chances, but they're worth takin', Lovin' might be a mistake, but it's worth makin',	I am taking chances on new and good things So my kids are happy and safe around me.
Don't let some hell-bent heart leave you bitter, When you come close to sellin' out reconsider,	Life may still make me angry. I will try to accept things and move on.
Give the heavens above more than just a passing glance,	I am hoping every day for something good

And when you get the choice to sit it out or dance,	And making a better life for myself.
I hope you dance– I hope you dance.	I am really changing ... I am going to dance.

In this case illustration, the MT chose song transformation as a means of engaging the client musically because of the affordances of this method-variation and of the choices that she had for structuring this experience to meet the client's needs while utilizing her strengths and abilities. She also wanted to facilitate the client's agency in determining her own therapeutic process. For example, the MT did not choose the song that would be used for the transformation but instead offered a selection that she knew would be useful for this type of experience. Likewise, she did not preselect which parts of the song were to be rewritten. The client's abilities did not require such a high level of structure, since she could read and write and did not have any apparent cognitive limitations that would make a low level of structure a contraindication for her participation.

The MT did, however, recognize some limitations in her readiness for change, as demonstrated by her inability to move beyond the difficult feelings and emotions she experienced in relation to her circumstances. This prompted the various choices that the MT made over time to challenge the client just enough to stimulate self-awareness and change without asking too much and causing the client to shut down, give up, or potentially stop attending sessions. As the client increased in her readiness to address more difficult therapeutic material, the MT concurrently adapted the experience structure and directives to maintain an appropriate level of challenge for the client and maintain the momentum in the client's therapeutic progress. In the end, the client almost completely rewrote the words to the song, retaining the melody, harmony, and approximate rhythmic structure of the original. This type of song transformation is referred to as a song parody (Baker & Wigram, 2005).

Literature Illustrating Song Transformation

Abbott (2018) describes the use of song transformation with a group of older adults who resided in a nursing facility. In this case, the members of the group had varying levels of ability as well as a range of limitations, including sensory and physical difficulties. Based on her knowledge of the needs of these individuals with whom she interacted on a regular basis, the MT selected a type of song transformation called piggyback songwriting (Baker & Wigram, 2005), in which words or selected phrases of the original song are replaced with others chosen by the clients. Piggyback songwriting provides a higher level of structure than does song parody since more of the original structure of the song is retained. The additional structure made this a good choice in this case because the MT needed to ensure that the experience allowed the participation of all of the group members despite their varying levels of ability. It also allowed her to preplan and prepare the needed materials the group would require to fully participate. These included song lyric sheets that had blanks in the places in the original song where the group could insert their own choices and a large white board on which the group's choices could be written. The MT also chose a song for this experience that she had sung together with this group on previous occasions, so its familiarity increased the ease with which the group could make the song their own.

In providing this higher level of structure for the group's song transformation, the MT simultaneously created opportunities for the group to freely choose what they wanted to express. Using clear directives and prompts that focused the group's discussion and decision-making (e.g., suggesting that they pick a theme for the song), the MT made no further decisions about the song content and instead acted as a scribe, writing down the group's ideas and words on the white board. Since the decision-making was placed on the group members, it also demanded that they interact with one another and collaborate to create the needed words and phrases to complete the song. After the MT assisted the group in fitting their words and phrases into the original song structure, they sang it together with the MT's accompaniment on guitar. The group then discussed what it was like to hear their own thoughts expressed in the new song, and they were able to identify how it was helpful to them. In closing the group session, the MT made sure that each had a song sheet that was fully completed with the new words.

The song transformation in this case was intended to be completed in one group session's time—another reason for the necessity of the MT's choice to provide a higher level of structure. In another case described by Krout (2011), a single-session format also necessitated preplanning with a level of structure that allowed for completion of the experience within the limited time available. This group involved adolescents who were bereaved and who had gathered as a group as a part of a 3-day family bereavement retreat. The MT had not worked with these teenagers prior to the event and had to rely on information from the families' intake applications for the retreat as a basis for his planning. He chose to precompose a song with lyrics that spoke directly to the experiences of the group members as recounted in the application materials. The MT's original song was then used as the vehicle for song transformation during the retreat music therapy session.

The MT performed his song for the group, using guitar for his accompaniment. He then facilitated a discussion with the teens about the lyrical content of the song. He offered the group the opportunity to change some of the lyrics in the song to more closely reflect their own personal thoughts, feelings, and experiences. The group brainstormed ideas, and the MT acted as scribe. Ensuring that everyone's suggestions were incorporated, the MT helped the group to fit their ideas into the form of the song. Most of the two verses were replaced with the group's new lyrics, as was half of the original chorus. To close the session, the MT offered the options of either performing the song live at the final remembrance service closing the retreat or recording it for the same purpose. The group chose to record the song and have the recording played, so the MT assisted in making the recording and provided the guitar accompaniment. The MT introduced and explained the significance of the song at the remembrance ceremony, and then the recording was played for the families in attendance. A recording was also given to each of the group members at the conclusion of the service.

In a chapter discussing theoretical perspectives on eating disorder treatment, McFerran and Heiderscheit (2016) offered a case illustrating a cognitive-behavioral approach that involved the song transformation method-variation. In this case, the MT recognized that an expressed realization of one group member was challenging the distorted beliefs of other group members and saw this as an opportunity to assist the clients in exploring those beliefs. She introduced songwriting to the group, and the group agreed to write a song on the topic using the melody from Johnny Nash's song "I Can See Clearly Now" to structure their ideas. The MT led the group in brainstorming around the topic, writing ideas on a white board so that the lyrics for the song could be pulled from these ideas. The group selected and arranged the words as lyrics for the song, and these too were written on the white board so that everyone could see the product as it came together and changes could be suggested and easily made. They performed the final version together, and the group expressed pride in their work and wanted to share it with staff at the facility. They also requested a written copy of the lyrics and a recording of its performance.

The MT in this case had not planned on engaging the group in songwriting in this session, but because this particular issue emerged as a primary need in the moment, she exercised flexibility by offering a method-variation that afforded the group members what they needed in order to explore, resolve, and integrate the issue at hand. This is an excellent example of how constant assessment and clinical decisions based on the needs of the client in the moment provide the most effective means of therapy, even in a setting in which treatment is based on a structured, behavioral approach. The MT was able to actively engage the group in a music process that, though not predefined, resulted in outcomes that were demonstrated within the music product. Understanding the affordances of songwriting, and song transformation in particular, allows for this kind of flexibility in clinical decision-making.

In another case (Heiderscheit, 2008), clients in a partial hospitalization treatment program for eating disorders requested to write a song about saying good-bye to their disorder. Their idea for writing this song transformation was inspired by their hearing the Dixie Chicks' song "Good-bye, Earl." The MT recognized that they had accessed their own sense of empowerment in requesting that they create a song in which they musically part from their disorder. The MT led the group in brainstorming their ideas, as in the case above. The final song reflected the course of their disorder from its beginning, through the impact on their lives, to treatment, and into their process of recovery. In this case, the MT was working from an experience orientation, as the clients were recognizing their needs in treatment and expressing their desire to explore them through music process. The MT's understanding of the affordances of song transformation and the structure of song transformation made it possible for the MT to act on the needs and wishes of the clients without having to preplan the experience.

Other Literature Related to Song Transformation

Interestingly, the literature on song transformation is quite sparse, considering that music therapists are likely to use this highly adaptable method-variation often and across a wide range of clients with varying abilities and therapeutic needs (Baker, Wigram, Stott, & McFerran, 2008). Some examples do exist, although they are largely about the process of the client or client group and do not necessarily reveal much about the thought processes or implementation choices of the MT. They do, however, provide other useful information if you are interested in digging deeper into this method-variation.

In two specific instances, song transformation was used as a part of a therapeutic process that also included other method-variations. Bates (2018) describes the use of song transformation with a woman undergoing a bone marrow transplant. The primary method used with this patient was re-creative, but in response to her needs as they emerged over the course of music therapy, a re-creative experience led into a transformation experience in which the music therapist assisted her in transforming a preferred precomposed song as the vehicle for exploring her experience in the hospital. Baker and Stretton-Smith (2018) utilized song transformation experiences to prepare a group of people with dementia to participate in the method-variation of songwriting. In this case, the structure of song transformation served as a primer, so to speak, that developed familiarity with and comfort in the compositional process that allowed the clients to be successful in participating in the less structured and more demanding experience of creating an original song. These examples reflect the usefulness of song transformations as transitions to or from other method-variations and highlight the flexibility of methods-based clinical decision-making to assist the music therapist in making choices that are the most effective for the needs of the client as they emerge in the moment.

Song transformation has been used as the treatment choice in some research studies. Ettenberger and Ardila (2018) utilized song transformation as an intervention choice for a study in which they examined the effectiveness of songwriting with mothers of preterm infants in a NICU setting. This study was designed from a positivist perspective and based on a traditional empirical design that required variables to be properly controlled. Song transformation was chosen as a treatment option within the protocol for the study, the results of which suggested that songwriting, in general, may indeed be beneficial for supporting the relationship between preterm infants and their mothers. In another study, Hong and Choi (2011) used song transformation experiences to study the impact of songwriting on the cognitive functioning of older adults with dementia. Song transformation was also used in an interpretivist study by Baker and Stretton-Smith (2018) that explored the perspectives of individuals with dementia who had participated in therapeutic group songwriting. Here the researchers used Interpretive Phenomenological Analysis to analyze the qualitative data related to the experience of songwriting. While there is little discussion of the method-variation itself in any of these studies, they demonstrate, though indirectly, how the structure that is particular to song transformation provides to people with significant limitations the affordances of a compositional process and how this same structure lends itself to the demands of research methodology.

There are several clinical articles that include song transformation as a recommended experience for clientele with particular kinds of needs. Some of these include women with addictions (Gardstrom, Carlini, Joselczyk, & Love, 2013), individuals with dissociative identity disorder (Gleadhill & Ferris, 2010), older adults in end-of-life (Hogan, 2003), and adolescents with cancer (Ledger, 2001). Additionally, there is a large body of literature identifying songwriting as a means for engaging music therapy clients. Often in these articles, however, it is not made clear whether the authors are referring to the method-variation of song transformation or that of songwriting. Nevertheless, if you are interested in understanding more about the affordances of song transformation, a perusal of this literature is worth your while for increasing your awareness of the myriad aspects involved in selecting and designing song transformation experiences for your clients.

Finally, the *Guidelines for Music Therapy Practice* series from Barcelona Publishers offers you excellent information about the use of song transformation from the perspective of the needs of various clientele groups and settings. These are highly recommended resources, and you are encouraged to use them to support your preparation process for selecting, designing, and implementing song transformation experiences. Chapters that include information specific to song transformation are identified by volume in the following tables.

Table 3.1
Guidelines for Music Therapy Practice in Mental Health
(Eyre, 2014)

Author	Chapter	Title
Hunt	2	Adults with Schizophrenia and Psychotic Disorders
Eyre	3	Adult Groups in the Inpatient Setting
Eyre	4	Adults in a Recovery Model Setting
Doak	5	Children and Adolescents with Emotional and Behavioral Disorders in an Inpatient Psychiatric Setting
Zanders	6	Foster Care Youth
Hatcher	9	Adult Male Survivors of Abuse and Developmental Trauma
Jackson	11	Adults with Depression and/or Anxiety
Dvorkin	12	Adults and Adolescents with Borderline Personality Disorder
Murphy	14	Adults with Substance Use Disorders
McFerran	15	Adolescents with Substance Use Disorders
Kaser	16	Adult Males in Forensic Settings
Melendez	17	Adult Females in Correctional Facilities
Gardstrom	18	Adjudicated Adolescents
Rea-Kolb	19	Juvenile Male Sex Offenders
Abbott	20	Elderly Residents in Nursing Facilities
Young	21	Persons with Alzheimer's Disease and Other Dementias
Brooks	22	Professional Burnout
Kim	23	Stress Reduction and Wellness
Trondalen	24	Musicians

Table 3.2
Guidelines for Music Therapy Practice in Pediatric Care
(Bradt, 2014)

Author	Chapter	Title
Whitehead-Pleaux	7	Burn Care for Children
Dun	8	Children with Cancer
Neugebauer	13	Children in General Inpatient Care

Table 3.3
Guidelines for Music Therapy Practice in Adult Medical Care
(Allen, 2014)

Author	Chapter	Title
Tamplin	4	Adults in Critical Care
Leist	5	Cardiac Care
Cohen	8	Adults with Neurogenic Communication Disorders
Keith	10	Adults with HIV/AIDS
Allen	11	Adults with Cancer

Table 3.4
Guidelines for Music Therapy Practice in Developmental Health
(Hintz, 2014)

Author	Chapter	Title
Schwartz	2	Early Intervention
Hintz	3	Autism
Sokira	4	Rett Syndrome
Hintz	7	Learning Disabilities in School Children
McCarrick	8	Behavioral and Interpersonal Problems in School Children

References

Abbott, E. (2018). Song transformation with older adults in a skilled nursing facility, In A. Heiderscheit & N. Jackson, *Introduction to Music Therapy Practice*. Barcelona Publishers.

Allen, J. (2014). *Guidelines for music therapy practice in adult medical care*. Barcelona Publishers.

Baker, F., & Wigram, T. (2005). *Songwriting: Methods, techniques and clinical applications for music therapy clinicians, educators, and students*. Jessica Kingsley.

Baker, F., Wigram, T., Stott, D., & McFerran, K. (2008). Therapeutic songwriting in music therapy. *Nordic Journal of Music Therapy, 17*(2), 105–123. https://doi.org/10.1080/08098130809478203

Baker, F. A., & Stretton-Smith, P. A. (2018). Group therapeutic songwriting and dementia: Exploring the perspectives of participants through interpretative phenomenological analysis. *Music Therapy Perspectives, 36*(1), 50–66. https://doi.org/10.1093/mtp/mix016

Bates, D. (2018). Re-creative music therapy in the midst of bone marrow transplant. In A. Heiderscheit & N. Jackson, *Introduction to Music Therapy Practice* (pp. 66–67). Barcelona Publishers.

Bradt, J. (2014). *Guidelines for music therapy practice in pediatric care*. Barcelona Publishers.

Ettenberger, M. & Ardila, Y. M. B. (2018). Music therapy song writing with mothers of preterm babies in the Neonatal Intensive Care Unit (NICU) – A mixed-methods pilot study. *The Arts in Psychotherapy, 58*(1), 42–52.

Eyre, L. (2014). *Guidelines for music therapy practice in mental health*. Barcelona Publishers.

Gardstrom, S. C., Carlini, M., Josefczyk, J., & Love, A. (2013). Women with addictions: Music therapy clinical postures and interventions. *Music Therapy Perspectives, 31*(2), 95–104. https://doi.org/10.1093/mtp/31.2.95

Gleadhill, L., & Ferris, K. (2010). A theoretical music therapy framework for working with people with dissociative identity disorder. *Australian Journal of Music Therapy, 21*, 42–55.

Heiderscheit, A. (2008). Discovery and recovery through music: An overview of music therapy with adults in eating disorder treatment. In S. Brooke (Ed.), *The creative therapies and eating disorders* (pp. 122–141). Charles C. Thomas Publishers.

Heiderscheit & N. Jackson, *Introduction to Music Therapy Practice* (pp. 66–67). Barcelona Publishers.

Hintz, M. (2014). *Guidelines for music therapy practice in developmental health*. Barcelona Publishers.

Hogan, B. E. (2003). Soul music in the twilight years: Music therapy and the dying process. *Topics in Geriatric Rehabilitation, 19*(4), 275–281. https://doi.org/10.1097/00013614-200310000-00008

Hong, I. S., & Choi, M. J. (2011). Songwriting-oriented activities improve the cognitive functions of the aged with dementia. *The Arts in Psychotherapy, 38*(4), 221–228. https://doi.org/10.1016/j.aip.2011.07.002

Krout, R. E. (2001). Our path to peace: Songwriting-based grief music therapy with bereaved adolescents. In A. Meadows (Ed.), *Developments in music therapy practice: Case study perspectives* (pp. 230–247). Barcelona Publishers.

Ledger, A. (2001). Song parody for adolescents with cancer. *Australian Journal of Music Therapy, 12,* 21–28.

McFerran, K. S., & Heiderscheit, A. (2016). A multi-theoretical approach for music therapy in eating disorder treatment. In A. Heiderscheit (Ed.), *Creative arts therapies and clients with eating disorders* (pp. 357–376). Jessica Kingsley.

4

SONGWRITING WITH INDIVIDUALS

Songwriting is a music experience in which the client composes an original song or any part of the song (e.g., lyrics, melody, accompaniment) with varying levels of technical support and assistance from you, the music therapist. The process includes some form of notation, such as writing out the lyrics and/or chords to the song and/or creating the notation of the song through a software program and may include making a recording of the final product. You assist the client in identifying the topic(s) for their song, writing the lyrics, determining the musical genre or style, writing the music, and creating a recording. This results in creating an original song and a personalized expression of what the client wants or needs to communicate or express. The song becomes a musical product the client can perform, share on the recording, and replay. The printed music, lyrics, and recording become an artifact that the client can keep. It can be utilized to review their therapeutic process, keep a record of their therapeutic progress, or share with others or as a gift to someone.

Prerequisites

There are some prerequisites for a client to be able to engage in the songwriting process. It is important to recognize that some of these can be mitigated by the way you adapt and tailor the process based on the needs, skills, strengths, and limitations of the client. Your understanding of the client, planning, and preparation of resources, as well as the working therapeutic relationship, can make songwriting an accessible method-variation for clients with a variety of limitations. A prerequisite for songwriting is that a client must have some receptive language skills to comprehend the directions you provide. The client must also be able to make decisions. A client with limited or no expressive language can respond by indicating a "yes" or "no" by pointing at words or pictures or use a communication device to express their thoughts and feelings, as well as to make decisions.

Risks and Contraindications

There are risks that can arise whenever you engage a client in trying something new or unfamiliar. This can foster feelings of inadequacy or a fear of failure in their ability to accomplish something they have never done before. A client may find it difficult to share their experiences or express their thoughts or feelings. This may cause them to feel vulnerable or uncomfortable, especially if they are expressing tender or intense emotions. Clients who have difficulty making decisions or are afraid that their choices won't result in the outcome they want might experience some frustration in the songwriting process.

These risks can be managed or minimized through thoughtful planning and providing the appropriate level of structure that supports the client in utilizing their strengths and accommodating any limitations. Your awareness of a client's potential risks in the songwriting process will allow you to recognize when difficulties may occur and be able to respond effectively to address and minimize these challenges.

Contraindications to songwriting are typically limited to a client who does not have language skills or a way to communicate or express their thoughts, ideas, or wishes. Songwriting may also be contraindicated if the client is disoriented or confused or has minimal consciousness. In these instances, clients not orientated to reality may struggle to organize their thoughts and ideas or have difficulty in expressing themselves in a meaningful way.

Affordances and Challenges

There are a variety of affordances innate in the songwriting process. There are also challenges in this process that you might utilize to help to address a client's therapeutic needs and process.

The choice of songwriting and how you structure the process for the client can provide unique affordances and challenges tailored to meet their needs and integrate their strengths and music preferences. The following affordances and challenges are common to the songwriting process. It is helpful to keep in mind that these affordances and challenges are not all-inclusive. The adaptations you make can allow for different affordances and challenges for the client. This allows you to implement their critical thinking and creativity to explore how to structure and tailor the process to best meet the needs of the client.

Decision-making. Writing a song is a process that is filled with a wide array of decisions. These include decisions about the lyrics, style or genre of music, form, tonality, instrumentation, and so forth. Some of these decisions may be new. Others may be unfamiliar to the client, so they may need information to make some of these decisions. For example, the client may want or need to hear different rhythms or rhythm patterns representative of variations genres so they can determine what may help to communicate the message in their lyrics. They may want to hear examples of different instruments to determine what instrumentation will help to convey the message of their song. It is important to engage the client in making decisions about the music so that they can feel a sense of ownership of their song. In some instances, a client may have a clear idea of what they want the song to sound like and can communicate this. This may include instrument, tonality, dynamics rhythm, and so on. It will be important to provide an opportunity for the client to hear the music and be able to make changes to it to help them best communicate their intention for the song. Clients who may be unsure of what they want musically may need support in making decisions about the music. They may need to hear some examples (such as genre, rhythm, modality, instrumentation, etc.) to decide what they want musically for their song.

Self-organization. The process of creating a song or any part of a song affords a client the opportunity to organize their own thoughts, feelings, and behaviors. This may take the form of writing song lyrics on a topic and creating verses and a chorus for a song that reflects their own life experiences. This process can challenge the client to focus on a task and to see it through to completion, allowing them to create something personal and meaningful.

Problem-solving. Creative experiences like songwriting engage a client's problem-solving skills. This may include the client choosing the words that they feel communicate and express their experiences most effectively, rhyming the ends of phrases, or finding the rhythm structure for a lyric. It may occur as the client reflects on aspects of their life they have included in the song and considers other choices they want to make in life.

Self-expression. Writing lyrics and music to create a song allows a client to express their own feelings, thoughts, and ideas. The process of writing and crafting lyrics and music allows them to choose the words and music that capture and communicate their feelings, thoughts, and ideas in the way they want them to be expressed. Creating their own song is an opportunity to communicate or share a message they want to convey for their own sake or that they want to articulate for others to hear. The lyrics and music may describe an experience or experiences the client wishes to describe.

Thematic exploration. Songwriting allows a client to focus their song on a topic related to their life or any aspect of their therapeutic process. Creating a song allows a client to focus on and explore their thoughts, ideas, and experiences. This can foster new awareness and insights in the respective area as they create something new and can listen to their own words within a musical structure.

Taking a risk and trying something new. Most clients do not have experience in creating a song. The various aspects of writing a song may be unfamiliar and, as a result, require a willingness to take a risk and to try doing something they have never done before.

Creating an artifact that documents one's life and process. The message in a song may be personal and serve to remind them of a new insight or discovery they want to share with others. This message may be a prompt to remember a significant experience from their life or therapeutic process. A client may choose to make a recording of their song. This allows the client to create an artifact, which is an item created utilizing the skill of the creator. The artifact is created for a particular purpose. Creating a song is producing an artifact that may represent a moment in one's life or life experiences or a process in one's life. This artifact is something to which the client can listen to again and again, reflecting not only on the process of creating and recording the song but also on what is documented in the song.

Sharing the creation that represents one's own experiences. Writing a song is an opportunity for the client to write about their topic of choice. This may include writing about their feelings, thoughts, or experiences. A key to this process is determining the way in which the client is best able to share this information. This can be communicated verbally or nonverbally. Clients may verbally communicate ideas they have about the topic of a song and then begin to craft lyrics that express their feelings, thoughts, ideas, and experiences as they relate to that topic. Clients who are nonverbal may use pictures or communication boards to communicate their ideas or to craft their lyrics. Making a recording and/or printed copies of the client's song allows them to share what they have created. A recording provides the opportunity for others to hear about the client's experiences and to hear about them in the client's own words and music.

Create a legacy to give to loved ones. A client may choose to create a song to give to someone or to several people whom they love. The song may communicate a message they want to share and that they want their loved ones to be able to listen to again and again. This could be a message they want to ensure that their loved ones have following their death, to be a legacy they leave or express thoughts or feelings they have found difficult to express in any other way.

Trust in the client–therapist relationship. Embarking on the process of trying something new requires that the client trust the therapist to guide and support the process. This necessitates a therapeutic rapport that fosters the client's sense of safety and security and that provides the support the client needs to try something new and different.

Work collaboratively. Engaging in an unfamiliar experience such as songwriting requires the client to work collaboratively with the therapist. The therapist brings expertise in creating a song and engages the knowledge, experience, and skills of the client. This collaborative process engages the client in communicating with the therapist and exploring ways of working together as ideas, opportunities, and options are shared.

Orientations to Clinical Decision-Making

Outcome Orientation

If you are working from an outcome orientation when engaging a client in songwriting, you will be considering how the process can assist the client in addressing specific treatment goals or objectives and therapeutic needs. These have typically been identified in the music therapy assessment or within the larger context of a program assessment. An outcome orientation experience may include engaging the client in expressing their thoughts and feelings, making decisions and choices, or engaging in a multistep process and completing each step to reach completion. Songwriting provides many different affordances and challenges that foster and support behavioral, cognitive, and social growth and development. In this process, music can serve different functions as it is used to address a therapeutic issue and affect change.

Music as agent. In the songwriting experience, music can function as a means to *stimulate* or *induce* a change in the body. This could include helping to relax the body, decrease pain, change a mood state, or support and foster movement. Utilizing songwriting to do this may include helping the client to write a song that they can sing at a slow tempo that would include lyrics that focus on the steps to slow their breathing and having the musical elements of the song (rhythm, tempo, melody, etc.) support taking slow, deep breaths; singing long phrases to support breath control; and fostering the relaxation response.

Music as skill. Engaging in songwriting requires the client to engage different skills, skills they may not use in other types of experiences. You may structure the experience to support a client working on a specific skill or skills. If a client can practice these skills in an enjoyable way, this can foster their engagement in the experience and therapeutic process. This could include a client who is working on practicing positive self-talk to reduce the negative or critical messages that they have internalized. The lyrics of the song the client creates can incorporate the positive messages the client wants and needs to hear. The music the client composes can support the lyrics to conjure positive emotions to support the client's experience of hearing the positive messages in the lyrics, which can help them to internalize these messages.

The songwriting process can elicit behaviors that may be important for the client to learn or practice. For example, writing a song requires a client to make choices. To create a song, there are decisions to make regarding the lyrics and the music; this process will require the client to engage in making choices to create their song. Music can also provide opportunities to *manage* behaviors. A client who has difficulty in expressing emotions in appropriate ways can explore how creating lyrics and music that express challenging emotions can be done in appropriate ways and in ways that may also allow others to hear what they are trying to express.

Music therapy protocols. The songwriting process can be structured and utilized as a treatment protocol that is based on what has been defined in the client's assessment. The process may include objectives that the client achieves over the course of several sessions. For example, a client may be working on improving communication skills and expressing their feelings.

The therapeutic process may include the following objectives: (1) Identify the feelings that are difficult to communicate, (2) Communicate what is challenging about expressing these emotions, (3) Write how you want to express these feelings. The client may complete this work in a five-session series, writing the lyrics and music that communicate a message they have been struggling to share with a loved one. They may also choose to record and share this with their loved ones. In this process, the outcomes are clearly delineated and defined. While the objectives of the process are nonmusical, the songwriting experiences provide a way for the therapeutic goal(s) to be accomplished through the music experience.

Experience Orientation

The use of songwriting from an experience-oriented perspective includes two primary considerations regarding what the songwriting process will provide for the client. It is important to recognize that these two perspectives are both a part of a client's songwriting process.

Music as process. In this perspective, the songwriting experience allows the client to engage in self-exploration or explore their life experiences. The process of crafting the lyrics can allow the client to reflect on their experiences and make new discoveries as they find the words that accurately capture these experiences. Creating the music that accompanies the lyrics can provide in-depth meaning to their words as they explore how the music helps to express the meaning of their words. Additionally, the client may discover new meaning in the process of creating their song. An example of this is a client in addictions treatment exploring their life experiences to understand what has led to the development of their addiction.

Music as representation. Creating a song provides an opportunity for the client to have a musical product. The product may include having the lyrics with the music notated or creating a recording or video. The song serves as a means to represent and reflect the client's experiences or processes. For example, this could be a child undergoing a bone marrow transplant (BMT) who creates a song that reflects on their experiences I navigating this complex treatment. Creating a product of the client's song allows them to listen to or watch it again and again and to share it with others. This can help the patient in reflecting on their process as they continue their transplant recovery, as well as to help others to understand what they have been through as a part of the journey.

Creating a musical product and having a tangible artifact may help the client to feel a sense of accomplishment at a time when they are not able to do anything else as a result of their treatment process.

General Considerations and Procedural Guidelines

When you have determined that songwriting is the music experience to best meet the client's needs and therapeutic goals, you will then plan, engage, implement, observe, and evaluate the effectiveness of this method-variation. The following are general procedures that address how songwriting would typically be facilitated. In each of these respective areas, it is vital to consider the client and adapt these procedures to allow the client to successfully engage in the experience. This may require you to think creatively as you explore and determine how to adapt the process for the client. There are a myriad of ways to adapt the songwriting process for clients to make the process accessible and to allow the client to be successful.

Planning: You will need to determine the client's specific skills, abilities, and limitations as they relate to engaging in the songwriting experience. These may include any of the following:

- Language and communication skills (verbal or nonverbal)
- Ability to read and write
- Cognitive abilities (concrete or abstract thinking)
- Physical limitations
- Ability to attend to a task (how long the client can focus)
- Ability to identify feelings
- Ability to recall and share their experiences
- Ability to express or communicate feelings
- Music preferences
- Music experiences
- Music knowledge

When you have determined the client's skills, abilities, and limitations, you will need to determine the level of structure needed to ensure the client can engage in the songwriting process.

- Do you need pictures, photos, or a communication device to allow the client to communicate the words they want for their lyrics?
- Can the client identify a topic or theme for their song?
- Can the client read their song lyrics to record or perform their song?
- Can the client write to share their ideas or to write their song lyrics?
- • Does the client play an instrument that they want to incorporate into their song?
- Are there instruments that the client prefers?

Next, you need to determine what materials will be needed in the songwriting process to write the lyrics and music and record or perform the song.

- Writing utensils: pen, pencil, or marker
- White board or paper to write down lyrics
- Pictures, photos, communication device
- Instruments
- Electronic equipment to produce beats or rhythms
- Laptop or tablet with software or program to record a song
- Camera to make a video recording
- Microphone

It is important to keep in mind that the materials you select may depend on the clinical setting you are in or that are available. For example, if you are working with a client in contact isolation on a medical unit, you will only be able to take in the materials that will stay in the room or that can be wiped down and sanitized after the session. If there are contact precautions or restrictions, you may need to let the client know what instruments are available for use for their song.

Engaging. The directions provided to the client to engage them in the songwriting process need to be tailored to their developmental and cognitive levels. Then you can do the following:

- Describe the songwriting experience to the client; tell them the purpose of the experience and what they will be asked to do in the process
- Identify a topic or theme that the song will be about
- Write these ideas on a white board or paper
- Write the lyrics *or* write the music (see Table 4.0)
- Support the client in exploring and determining what they want to express and communicate about the theme or topic; provide minimal assistance in prompting or asking questions
- Allow the client to play the music as they are able
- Sing and play their song (if the client wants)
- Ask whether the client wants to make any changes to the lyrics or music
- Make a recording of the song

The process of composing a song can start with either the lyrics or the music. The process in which a song is created may be determined by how this method-variation is introduced into the therapeutic process. Both processes of song composition will be described in this section.

Table 4.0
Song Composition Process

Starting with the Lyrics	Starting with the Music
The client may come to the session with an idea or theme for a song that they would like to write.	The client may have a musical idea that they want to use as the basis of the music for a song. This musical idea may be from music that they have heard or music that they improvised or created.
Brainstorm and explore topics or themes to determine what the client wants to express and communicate.	Example: An adolescent has heard a rap whose rhythm they like and wants to create a similar beat and a composition based on that rhythm.
Engage the client in sharing their experience(s) to help to provide additional information and material for the lyrics. For example: If the client	Explore different musical ideas, helping the client to determine what they want or need to hear musically. This may include exploring genre,

chooses to write a song about their experience of getting a transplant, you may brainstorm with them on what they want to express or communicate, what the process was like, what helps them in the process of recovery, what they want others to know, and so forth.	style, rhythm patterns, instrumentation, mode, tonality, dynamics, and so on. It may be helpful to provide musical examples for the client to hear to help them make decisions regarding the music.
Write the client's ideas on paper or a white board.	Determine whether the client wants to play one or more instruments as a part of their song composition. Decide in collaboration with the client what you will play.
Determine an order for the ideas shared, which will help to provide the outline for the song lyrics.	Play the completed musical composition. Ask the client if there are any changes that they want to make to the music.
Assist the client in generating the lyrics of their song, writing them down on paper or a white board. The process may start with writing a verse or writing the chorus for their song.	Explore with the client what the music communicates and what they want to express in the lyrics.
The client may make decisions regarding the number of verses included in their song, based on what they want to communicate.	Write these ideas on paper or a white board. It may be helpful to ask the client questions to clarify and explore these topics, ideas, and words.
The chorus may remain the same between each verse, it may be alerted slightly, or it may be different each time.	Support the client in formulating these ideas and words into phrases that will formulate their lyrics and chorus.
When the song lyrics are completed and the client does not want to make any further changes, you can begin to explore what is needed in the music to support the expression of the lyrics.	Assist the client in developing their lyrics in the way that they want them to fit within the structure and form of the music that they created.
Discuss and explore with the client what they want to hear in the music to support the message in their lyrics. This may include exploring genre, style, instrumentation, mode, tonality, dynamics, and so on. Provide musical examples if needed.	Play the music created and sing each new lyric or phrase created to ensure that the client can decide that it is written in the way that they want to hear it. Continue this process until the lyrics and chorus are completed.

Allow the client to make decisions regarding the music to ensure that they maintain ownership of their song.	Determine if the client wants to make any additional changes musically or to the lyrics of their song.
When the music is completed, play and sing the song with the client. Determine whether the client wants any additional changes made to their song.	

Observing. Pay attention to the time and effort that the client is needing and putting into the songwriting experience. You can provide prompting and make adjustments as needed throughout the process.

- Is the client generating ideas for a topic or theme?
- Do they have a musical idea with which they want to start?
- Do they need some prompting to come up with ideas?
- Is the client able to problem-solve during the process?
- Is the client experiencing any difficulties or frustration in the process?
- Are any thoughts or feelings being elicited in the process?
- Does the client need support to explore their thoughts or feelings further to write about them?
- How is the client reacting to what they are creating?

Adapting. The assistance a client needs will depend on their skills, abilities, development, and music experience. Most clients have not engaged in songwriting before, so they will likely need assistance in how to begin. A client may decide to sing or play their song, or they may want you to sing and play it. If the client plays an instrument, this requires being able to incorporate that instrument into the music accompaniment. If the client does not have training on an instrument, consider what they can play as a part of their musical accompaniment. This may include playing a rhythm-based instrument, using color-coded keys, playing the guitar with an open tuning, and so forth. Providing the opportunity for the client to be a part of playing and singing their song gives them a greater sense of ownership of their song and a sense of accomplishment and empowerment, especially if they have never composed and recorded a song before.

By choice or because they are nonverbal, a client may decide they want a recording of their song but do not want to sing or play it. Or, a client may want you to sing and play their song. In this instance, it is important to allow the client to make musical decisions regarding their song to ensure they have a sense of ownership of their song. They can engage in making decisions that impact the production and outcome of their song.

Developing. This process is multifaceted in that it includes the development of the song. The client may develop new ideas, insights, and content for their song throughout the song composition process. First and foremost, it is important to recognize that the song composition belongs to the client. Therefore, supporting the client in developing their song is important. In the process of creating the lyrics, this may include asking the client questions or providing prompts to help them to generate their thoughts and ideas or to find the words to express their feelings. This process may continue as the client engages in creating the music to accompany their lyrics. It is important to explore how the music can support what is being expressed and communicated in the client's song. The client may want or need to hear examples to be able to make a decision. It may be helpful for them to hear different keys (including major or minor), genres and styles, and instrumentation to explore how these different musical elements can support the expression of their lyrics.

The client may choose to play an instrument and to sing their song. Supporting the client in finding a way to actively sing and play their song can further develop their relationship with their song and their ability to express what they hope to be communicated in their own words. The client may or may not want you to sing with them. There are also options in how the client may choose to have the music therapist engage in their song:

- The client sings and plays accompaniment alone
- The client sings alone, you play accompaniment
- Client and you sing in unison
- The client sings the melody, you sing harmony or backup vocals
- The client sings the melody and records harmony, and tracks are mixed

The musical choices should be based on what the client wants for their song and what will help them to express and communicate the intended message in their song.

Accompanying. If the client chooses to sing and play their song, it is important that what you play supports what the client is playing, is consistent with what the client has chosen, and does not overpower what the client is playing. If the client chooses not to play or sing their song, it is your responsibility to play what the client hopes to hear in their song. In this process, you can provide the client with different musical choices and options to allow them to decide how you accompany their song. In this process, it is helpful if you can highlight and share what you hear in the client's music and play different musical sounds that can support what they are striving to express or communicate.

Reviewing. When the lyrics and music for the song are completed, it is helpful to play and sing the song to allow the client to hear their completed composition. This is an opportunity for the client to hear their song in its entirety and to determine if there are any changes they want to make. When they are satisfied with their song, it is important to allow the client time to reflect on the process. It is helpful to understand the client's experience of the songwriting process. There are questions you may consider asking the client to review the process and understand their experience. The questions you ask will be tailored to the client's own experience, therapeutic process, skill, and developmental level. Some questions you may consider include:

- How do you feel, knowing that you created your own song?
- How does it feel to hear your own words in the song?
- How did you feel when you sang the song you created?
- How did you feel after hearing the song you created?
- What did you enjoy about the process?
- What was challenging about the process?
- Is there anything you would like to do with your song?

Based on how the client responds, there may be other questions that you ask. As you listen deeply to the client's response and observe their affect, ask the questions that come to mind for you, as these will be authentic questions that will be relevant to the client's experience and process.

Closing. You may end the session by processing the client's experience of creating the song. You may also ask if the client would like to sing or hear their song one more time and allow the session to close with their song. This allows you as the therapist to provide the opportunity for the client to make a choice in the session. This can also be a way to honor and validate their work by closing the session with their creation.

Creating a recording of a client's song provides them with an artifact of what they created that they can keep, listen to again and again, and share or give to others. It is important to provide the client the opportunity to decide whether they want to create a recording of their song. The client may have a preference to record only audio or to make a video recording. This decision may also be determined by the equipment available for use in making recordings. There is a wide array of technology available that is easily accessible, such as recording the video on a client's phone or tablet. There are also various technologies that can be used to create a more nuanced and crafted recording or video. Chapter 12 is dedicated to exploring the use of technology in compositional methods.

Special Considerations

This section focuses on special considerations for clients in different age groups. While these considerations are generalized to different age groups, it is important that they be tailored to each client whom you may encounter and that you recognize that these considerations can vary greatly within each age group, as well as across the life span. These considerations focus on aspects that vary from the general considerations explored previously in the chapter. They do not cover every aspect that you may need to recognize and understand, as clients are unique and need to be valued and understood as the individuals whom they are—with their own strengths, knowledge, skills, talents, interests, needs, and experiences.

With children. Given that children can vary significantly in their skills, abilities, and developmental stages, it is important to assess a child. The way in which you engage one child in the process may vary from how you engage another child, as you will need to adapt how you engage a 5-year-old in songwriting as compared to how you engage a 10-year-old in the experience. Overall, children have not yet developed skills in abstract thinking, so this will influence how you plan and structure the songwriting experience. You will need to consider the level of structure the client needs to successfully engage in the process. For younger children, this might mean keeping the lyric phrases short and structured, including repetition in the song form, and considering what instrument(s) the child can play or how you can adapt instruments for the child. Children have a smaller vocal range, so melodies for their song need to work within this range. Melodies should also move in a stepwise fashion or use small intervals or leaps to accommodate their vocal skills. Reading and writing skills may be limited or not yet developed. It will be helpful to consider the use of visual aids to assist in the songwriting process.

With adolescents. Identity formation is a key developmental stage for adolescents. As a result, adolescents may feel vulnerable, struggle with their own identity, and be concerned about judgments by and perceptions of others. This process is also influenced by various aspects that inform their identity, including culture, gender identity and expression, race, socioeconomic status, and religion. As a result, it is important to create a sense of safety throughout the songwriting process to support the client's sense of comfort in being able to share their music preferences, express their emotions, and disclose challenges they have encountered.

With older adults. Older adult clients may experience different physical problems and sensory issues due to the aging process. These can include decreased vocal range, vision, hearing, and physical dexterity (fine and gross motor movement). Assessing their physical and sensory skills will provide the information needed to determine the preparations and adaptations needed for the songwriting process. While older adults may have strong language skills, they may have difficulty in recalling information, reading, and writing. Writing lyrics in large or bold print on paper or a white board can help to ensure they can see their lyrics. Older adults typically lose hearing in the upper registers, and their vocal range becomes limited as well. Melodies for songs should not have a large vocal range and will need to be in a lower key to accommodate their vocal register.

Conclusion

For clients in the therapeutic process, songwriting provides a plethora of unique affordances and opportunities, many of which are distinctive to the songwriting experience. It is important to understand what the songwriting process has to offer clients to make clinical decisions about the use of this method-variation. Additionally, determining the orientation of the experience is vital in the client's therapeutic process. As we understand the intention of the songwriting experience and the therapeutic needs it can address, this provides information about how the experience will be oriented. Then, as we plan and prepare for this music experience, there are many different considerations specific to the songwriting process and unique to the client that we need to explore. Understanding these considerations helps the MT to plan, prepare, facilitate, and support the client throughout the songwriting experience. These considerations illustrate the number and variety of clinical decisions that an MT makes before and during the songwriting process. They also highlight the importance of the MT's critical thinking skills and creativity to shape and facilitate this compositional method-variation.

Reference

Bruscia, K. (2014). *Defining music therapy* (3rd ed.). Barcelona Publishers.

5

INDIVIDUAL SONGWRITING — ILLUSTRATIONS AND EXAMPLES IN THE LITERATURE

Songwriting with a Pediatric Intensive Care Patient

Ari was born with a heart defect and many other physical health complications that required her to use a wheelchair, maintain regular medical care, and undergo physical therapy. She was admitted to the pediatric intensive care unit (PICU) following a cardiac episode that left her unconscious and not breathing for several minutes. Since her body was without oxygen for this period of time, her fingers and toes lost circulation, which caused irreparable damage. The medical treatment team determined that all of her fingers and toes needed to be amputated to avoid causing serious infection in her body. The medical team referred Ari for music therapy to provide support and help her to process her emotions surrounding this upcoming medical procedure, as this was very difficult information to process emotionally at 10 years old.

The music therapist (MT) was asked to have a session with Ari in the morning, as that afternoon her family would be coming in and the child life specialist would be working with all of them to make prints of her hands and feet. The MT went to Ari's room and introduced herself. She conducted a brief assessment and asked Ari if there were anything in particular that she wanted to do in music therapy that day. In this clinical setting, the MT is often meeting the client for the first time at the time of the session and, as a result, is not able to do any planning before the session. The MT shared that she knew Ari would be undergoing a difficult medical procedure later in the week and that there was a ceremony planned for the coming afternoon as well. The MT chose to share this because it provided the opportunity to observe how Ari responded and would help her to assess whether Ari might be interested in addressing this in the music therapy session. Ari did share that she wanted to be able to express and communicate her feelings.

The MT identified songwriting as a choice because it would allow Ari to write lyrics that used her own words and would express and communicate what she wanted to say. The songwriting process would also afford Ari opportunities to make decisions that would empower her at a time when so many aspects of her treatment were outside of her control. The MT shared the idea of songwriting with Ari, who expressed excitement in creating an original song. The MT decided to begin the songwriting process with a focus on the lyrics, as Ari had previously indicated that she wanted to be able to express and communicate her feelings. Additionally, what Ari decided to write and the words she chose would likely influence her musical choices for her song.

The MT asked Ari to share her thoughts and ideas so she could understand what Ari wanted to express and communicate. The MT wrote them down so they could both look at Ari's words and begin to find connections in what she shared. The MT observed that Ari's ideas reflected many different activities and experiences that involved her fingers and toes. The MT discussed and reflected on this observation with Ari, and, in this conversation, Ari shared that she wanted to thank her fingers and toes for all of the things they had allowed her to do. She also disclosed that she recognized she needed to say good-bye to them. The MT recognized that the structure of the song could provide the platform through which Ari could give thanks for and acknowledge all that her fingers and toes had done. The MT presented to Ari the idea that she could use the chorus, which would be repeated after each verse, as her good-bye, while the verses could be the acknowledgment of and thank you to her fingers and toes.

Ari wondered whether the chorus could be the introduction of her song because she felt that was an important practice for her to focus on acknowledging the loss. The MT observed in this request that Ari felt safe and secure enough in the therapeutic process to ask and advocate for what she wanted for herself and her song. The MT let her know that the structure of the song could be adapted in whatever way Ari wanted. When the MT asked Ari what she wanted the chorus to communicate, she expressed the following:

> *Good-bye my fingers, good-bye my toes*
> *Good-bye my fingers, good-bye my toes*

The MT returned to the list they had created that described all of the activities and experiences of which Ari's fingers and toes had been a part. The MT asked Ari to group them in pairs of two to provide a structured way to create the verses. Each verse included two lines, and each line acknowledged one of the ways in which her fingers or toes had helped her. The MT then took these pairs of topics and asked Ari how she wanted to phrase each line. This allowed Ari to craft the verse by using her own words. As Ari created each line, the MT reflected on these different experiences with Ari. The process of reminiscing also allowed Ari to express her feelings and acknowledge her grief. Ari created three verses using the topics she had identified. When the verses were completed, the chorus was added at the beginning of the song and in between each verse. The MT asked Ari if this was the structure she wanted, and when that decision was finalized, it was time to create the music.

The MT talked with Ari about her musical choices for her song by showing her the instruments available, which were limited to what could be included on a cart and wheeled from room to room. Ari was not familiar with many of the instruments, so she was challenged in identifying sounds that matched what she wanted to express musically in her song. So, the MT asked Ari if there was a mood or overall feeling that best represented her lyrics. The MT recognized that if she understood the emotion or mood that Ari wanted to express in her song, this would provide the information needed to help to determine the type of instrumental and tonal sounds that Ari might want. Ari shared that she felt the song was tender and a little sad. The MT explored different instruments to let Ari hear the sounds and to begin to find what she felt captured the mood of her song. Ari selected the guitar.

The next step was creating the melody for the song. The MT played short and simple melody lines in different modes so that Ari could hear them and choose what she felt captured the emotion and essence of her song. The MT provided melody lines that followed stepwise movement or small leaps because Ari had indicated that she liked to sing but had not done a lot of it and did not feel she had a strong voice.

The MT was aware of the very intimate and personal nature of the song and knew that it was important for Ari to feel she could sing it. The MT sang melody samples and provided opportunities for Ari to make choices in creating the melody line. When the melody line was completed, the MT played the accompaniment on the guitar as she and Ari sang her song together. After they sang it, the MT reflected with Ari on her process of creating her song. Ari said she felt proud of what she had been able to create and felt brave from expressing these thoughts and feelings, and she asked whether the song could be a part of the ceremony in the afternoon with her family, as she wanted to share her song with them at the close of it. The MT consulted the child-life specialist and communicated Ari's request. Ari's song was integrated into the ceremony, which was videotaped at Ari's request. After Ari had completed making molds of her feet and hands, she and the MT sang her song;

> *Good-bye my fingers, good-bye my toes*
> *Good-bye my fingers, good-bye my toes*
>
> *You've helped me brush my hair and brush my teeth*
> *You've helped me tickle my baby brother to make him laugh*
>
> *Good-bye my fingers, good-bye my toes*
> *Good-bye my fingers, good-bye my toes*
>
> *You've helped me do my homework to write and learn*
> *You've helped color and painted pictures, too*

Good-bye my fingers, good-bye my toes
Good-bye my fingers, good-bye my toes

You've helped me paint my nails so many different colors
You've helped me eat my favorite snacks and food

Thank you, my fingers, thank you my toes
Good-bye my fingers, good-bye my toes
(Repeat last two lines)

 Singing and sharing the song with her family afforded Ari the opportunity to share her experiences and feelings related to this loss and help her family to better understand how she was working to process this difficult experience. Ari was tearful after sharing her song with her family, and she discovered that expressing and then sharing her feelings and experiences with others helped her to grieve and allowed others to know how she was feeling and when she needed their support. The MT talked with Ari and her family about recording the song during the ceremony so they could keep the artifact and Ari could listen to it in the future to reflect on this experience, honor her journey, and be reminded of her courage in the process.

 In this case illustration, the MT selected the method-variation of songwriting because it afforded Ari a way to express her feelings, make decisions, and foster her sense of agency. The MT understood the significance of these affordances because of the magnitude of the loss that Ari would experience in undergoing the procedure to amputate her fingers and toes. The MT observed that Ari demonstrated good verbal and communication skills in the brief assessment and expressed a desire to be able to express her feelings in her own way. Creating an original song provided Ari the opportunity to use her own words, to collaborate with the MT in selecting the instrumentation that expressed her ideas, and to co-create the music to accompany her lyrics. When challenges in the process arose that were beyond Ari's capabilities, such as choosing the accompanying instrument or discomfort with singing her song aloud, the MT adapted and provided structure to support and foster Ari's engagement. The observations that the MT made throughout the process helped to inform clinical decisions such as recognizing Ari's readiness to express her feelings of grief and loss, selecting the method-variation, and determining how the form of the song could support what Ari wanted to communicate.

Literature Illustrating Songwriting with Individuals

MTs adapt method-variations to address the unique needs of clients and to support their engagement in the music experience. In this section, three clinical cases of the use of songwriting with individual clients will be examined, with a focus on the decisions that the MT makes in planning, designing, implementing, and facilitating this method-variation. These case illustrations also demonstrate how the decisions that the MT makes provide the level of structure the client needs to effectively engage in the music experience through their therapeutic process.

Rolvsjord (2005) details the use of songwriting with a young adult female in her early 20s undergoing treatment in a mental health facility. The client entered treatment to address the trauma related to growing up in a home with a mother who was mentally ill and a father who was violent. The MT began the music therapy process by singing songs because the client wanted to reclaim singing, which had been a significant part of her life. The MT recognized that the client's cultural background had fostered a familiarity and degree of competence related to songs that in turn had fostered her development of a popular and folk song repertoire. This was evident in the easy and comfortable way in which she engaged musically. Building on these resources, the MT suggested they could create songs that integrated the client's own words, feelings, and experiences. The MT recognized that composing the music for lyrics provides new affordances; as the client makes decisions and choices about the musical elements and how to express their emotion in the lyrics, she becomes more emotionally engaged with the song.

The MT began the songwriting process by asking the client to write a few words or sentences about her feelings or experiences and bring them to the next sessions. This allowed the MT to observe and assess the client's capability to create lyrics and ascertain the level of structure and support the client may have needed to foster her engagement. In this case, the client soon began to bring in entire poems she had written that expressed her emotions of loneliness, anxiety, and despair; her wishes; and her messages of hope. The MT suggested that the client write in her own words her ideas about making choices regarding what to write about and provided the opportunity for the client to demonstrate her skill and competence in creating a narrative about her feelings and experiences. This challenge also allowed the MT to assess the readiness of the client to address her feelings and experiences. The choices the client made regarding what to write about would indicate what she was ready to bring to share with the therapist.

Throughout the therapeutic process, the client and therapist collaborated in creating over 30 songs. The client did not feel competent in creating the music but was capable of exploring and discussing musical options provided by the MT. Therefore, the MT structured the process by utilizing the client's poems and between sessions created a melody that expressed the emotion in the poems. The MT would play and sing the song created from the client's poem and then would collaborate with the client in making changes to the musical elements or the structure of the song based on the client's input and preferences. In the collaborative process, the MT provided musical options that required the client to make choices about the musical elements that she felt expressed her poem musically. Over time, this structured process supported the client in developing musical competence, and the MT could then explore different affordances available in the music to support the client's growth and development.

Gradually, the MT integrated improvisation into the songwriting process to provide new opportunities, demands, and challenges for the client. In one session, the MT and client selected a simple chord progression and improvised the lines of one of the client's poems by taking turns. In this collaborative process, they listened to each other, were inspired by each other's expressions, and created the song through a mutual and dynamic process. The different challenges the MT placed before the client in this process created opportunities for the client to engage with the music and MT in new ways. The MT observed the changes in the client's musical competencies during the therapeutic process and transitioned to utilizing different levels of musical engagement to provide the demands and challenges needed to foster the client's growth and development.

This case illustrates the decisions the MT made based on the client's available skills and resources. It also models that as a client develops their competence and skills, the MT can access new affordances, opportunities, demands, and challenges in the songwriting experience by adapting the way in which the client engages with the music. The MT evolved the challenges to support the client in developing her ability to express and communicate her feelings, to tolerate and work through challenging emotions, and to develop her identity, musical strengths, and resources.

Jackson (2018) describes the use of songwriting with a 5-year-old boy who had experienced neglect and undernourishment during his first 6 months of life. The client was 5 years old when his grandmother brought him for music therapy. The client was demonstrating difficulties with authority, having extreme temper tantrums, hitting and kicking others, and destroying property at home and at school. He appeared to have a lack of understanding of the impact of his behaviors on others. At the start of music therapy, the MT and the client agreed that their work would focus on recognizing his feelings of anger before they became overwhelming and to develop skills that he could use to help himself diffuse and resolve these emotions. The MT understood that recognizing intense emotions is easier than managing them. She initiated this therapeutic work by asking the client to improvise and make sounds that represented these feelings. This afforded him the space to explore and discover sounds that captured the essence of his emotions.

The next task was fostering the client's ability and skill in identifying appropriate ways to respond to these emotions. The MT recognized that this was a more challenging task for the client, considering his cognitive abilities were in the concrete operational stage of development. The MT understood this would necessitate framing his behaviors in terms of what the outcomes would be from the choices he makes. The MT created a simple repetitive melody that included verses composed of four incomplete phrases. This provided a structure in which the client could fill in words and phrases that served to remind him of what he should and should not do. Each verse he composed identified a different behavior and the typical consequences he would receive. This song structure and compositional format empowered the client to make his own choices and to include the skills on which he was working in school. He also included a plan for what to do when he got mad. Creating his song provided him a with resource that he could sing and use in the music therapy sessions, at home, and in school. The words he composed reminded him of the consequences of his poor choices and of different choices he could make. The choices he made in the songwriting process were an opportunity to practice and discover he could make his own choices that resulted in positive outcomes in his daily life.

This case models how an MT can provide a higher level of structure in songwriting to support the engagement of a young client. The repetitive melody provided the structure and simplicity appropriate for the client's cognitive and musical skill level. Filling in words and phrases provided the client with the opportunity to make choices in the therapeutic process and to exercise agency. He was then able to apply these skills in his life outside the context of the music therapy sessions.

Lewis (2019) details the individual songwriting process in his work with three different adult clients diagnosed with intellectual disabilities. The clients ranged in age from 33 to 67 years old, and each had a moderate intellectual disability. Songwriting was identified as the method-variation for use with these clients in order to offer opportunities to engage their agency as they determined the lyrical and musical content of their songs. Each client engaged in an individual songwriting process, with the MT providing a common structure for each of their respective processes. The process began with the MT utilizing a semi-structured format that allowed the client and therapist to collaborate in creating first the lyrics of the song and then the musical content, and then in producing a recording. Each session began with the MT introducing songwriting as a potential music experience. Then, following consent by the client to engage, the MT asked the client open-ended questions to generate ideas for a theme for the song. The open-ended questions engaged each client in identifying their interests and exploring any associations. As the clients shared their interests and experiences, the MT took notes of what the client shared in their session. The MT responded reflexively to responses from the clients and moment-to-moment changes in mood or affect in the sessions and throughout the process. The notes of the clients' own words and phrases that the MT generated were then used to generate the song lyrics.

When the song lyrics were completed, the client explored and experimented with playing various instruments in the music therapy room and then selected the instrument they wanted to play. Next, the client was given choices regarding the musical structure and content for their song. These choices included determining musical elements such as tempo (fast or slow) and mood (happy or sad). The MT played examples of different chord progressions to let the client hear them in order to then make their musical choices from various music genres and styles. In the process, the MT responded reflexively based on the client's affective and musical responses. After the client had made their musical choices, the MT and client then sang and played the song, after which the client was then asked if they wanted to make any changes. Each client could then decide if they wanted to make a recording of their song.

In the description of each client's respective process, the MT described the topics of each client's song; their song topics ranged from listening to country music to an upcoming transition, to money. The process of rehearsing and recording their songs was also a reflexive process, in which the MT adapted and tailored the musical structure and elements to support the client's ability to sing and play their song and their desired outcome.

These three cases on the use of individual songwriting with adults with intellectual disabilities illustrate how the MT can use a common format and structure in the process, how it can still be tailored to engage the clients' agency through allowing them to make decisions and choices for their song, and how various aspects of the process can be adapted to challenge and meet the unique needs and preferences of each client. They also illustrate what informs the MT's decisions for this method variation, how the MT process was structured to address the therapeutic needs of the client, the opportunities that this method-variation provided for the client, and the different ways in which the MT tailored the experience to foster and support the client's engagement. Other cases in the literature serve as examples of ways to structure and adapt songwriting for individual clients as well. Baker et al. (2005) describe how songwriting was integrated into the rehabilitative process for a 19-year-old client who had suffered a traumatic brain injury (TBI). This case models how songwriting allowed the client to exercise his sense of agency in expressing his feelings of anger, loss, and grief and supported the client's history of engaging in creative processes.

Rogers (2014) and Heiderscheit (2018a) explore how songwriting can address the therapeutic needs of clients who have experienced neglect, abuse, or trauma by fostering a sense of safety through the structure provided and how the song becomes a container and a vehicle for expressing difficult emotions. Murphy (2014) provides an adaptation and structure for individual songwriting within a group setting. This five-step process details how the MT can engage each client in the group to compose their song and share it within the context of the group. Abbott (2014) describes considerations for preparation, procedures, what to observe, and adaptions for songwriting with elderly residents in nursing facilities. Christy (2017) depicts initiating the songwriting process with clients with diagnosed Parkinson's disease and throughout the therapeutic process, integrating family members and caregivers into sessions. Heiderscheit (2018b) illustrates how songwriting can emerge from an improvisation experience, demonstrating how to transition from one method-variation to another.

There are a plethora of clinical illustrations, descriptions, and suggestions for the use of songwriting with a wide array of clientele. Table 5.0 includes a brief description of each case and details about which aspects of the songwriting process the case focuses on. Citations are also included to provide the information in case you want to read the full article or book chapter.

Table 5.0
Case Examples of Individual Songwriting in the Literature

Description of Case	Focus of Case	Reference
Songwriting via Skype with a 15-year-old diagnosed with Asperger's syndrome.	The case describes the technology utilized to conduct the songwriting sessions and examines the structure of therapeutic elements that supported and fostered the client's engagement.	Baker & Krout, 2009
Description of the structure for the songwriting process	Analysis of the themes that song lyrics yielded and how	Bradt, Biondo, & Vaudreuil,

for 11 active-duty service members diagnosed with PTSD.	songwriting provided the opportunity for service members to share their experiences, thoughts, feelings, fears, and hopes.	2019
Songwriting with an 18-year-old with a history of physical and sexual abuse.	Description of the structure and procedures MT utilized for songwriting sessions, with the emotions expressed in the songs with the song lyrics included.	Lindberg, 1995
Use of songwriting with a 17-year-old diagnosed with muscular dystrophy.	This case demonstrates how songwriting is utilized to establish and develop the therapeutic relationship, as well as to provide the opportunity for the client to receive emotional support.	Dwyer, 2007
Review of 17 songs written by three different adult clients living with serious mental illness.	Review of the songs created by the clients illustrates how they perceive and interpret their mental illness, as well as the catalysts that they describe in their songs that promote recovery for them.	Kooij, 2009
Songwriting with a transgender youth undergoing cancer treatment.	Exploration of how songwriting allowed the client to foster and strengthen intrapersonal and interpersonal relationships, as well as reframe his treatment process.	Beuchel, 2018
Songwriting with children and adolescents in inpatient psychiatric setting.	Considerations for preparing the environment to create a sense of safety and suggestions for how to structure sessions and tools to support creative and musical engagement and tools to foster creativity.	Doak, 2014; Johnson & Rickson, 2018

Use of songwriting with children and adolescents involved in the welfare system.	Discussion of how songwriting can be used as a psychological resource and to approach dealing with emotions and emotional issues that emerge in the songwriting process.	Zanders, 2014
Clinical considerations and structures needed when using songwriting with women and men survivors of abuse developmental trauma.	Overview of the considerations and structures needed to create a safe therapeutic space for trauma survivors to engage in songwriting. Discussion of the unique therapeutic issues that can also be addressed for clients with trauma in the process.	Curtis, 2014; Hatcher, 2014
Structuring songwriting experience for adults with depression and/or anxiety.	Discussion of ways to change and adapt the structure for the songwriting experience and how to transition from another method-variation into a songwriting experience.	Jackson, 2014
Adaptations and ways to structure the songwriting experience for clients with eating disorders.	Description of songwriting to create a song that serves as a protocol for self-care.	Tileston, 2014
Structuring the songwriting process for women in correctional facilities.	Exploration of the structure and support (musical and nonmusical) needed to foster client engagement.	Melendez, 2014
Considerations in use of songwriting with adjudicated youth.	Review of structure and facilitation of songwriting with and without various technology tools and products. Suggestions on what to observe throughout the songwriting process.	Gardstrom, 2014
Facilitating and structuring songwriting for individuals experiencing burnout and managing stress and to	Overview of ways to structure and facilitate the songwriting process and the different therapeutic goals that can be	Brooks, 2014; Heiderscheit, 2014a; Kim, 2014

foster well-being and engage as a means of spiritual practice.	addressed. Suggestions for resources that can be integrated into the songwriting process (poetry, journaling, scripture, etc.).	
Songwriting formats to utilize with children with cancer.	Descriptions of different formats that can be utilized and suggestions for structuring songwriting with children.	Dun, 2014; Marin, 2014
Songwriting process with adults in palliative and/or hospice, as a means of sharing their own story.	Details about how to structure the songwriting process to integrate a client's story.	Hilliard & Justice, 2011; Clements-Cortés, 2014
Songwriting as a means for self-expression and to facilitate transitions in pediatric medical and intensive care and for procedural support.	Suggestions and variations on ways to structure the songwriting experience to foster self-expression, support coping, and identify strengths and supports.	Ghetti; 2014; Mondanaro, 2014; Neugebauer, 2014
Therapist-assisted songwriting with children and adults with traumatic brain injuries (TBI).	Discussion of the structure, sequential order, and supports needed for clients with a TBI to engage in songwriting.	Street, 2012; Kennelly, 2014; Vega, 2014; Roddy et al., 2018
Songwriting with adults as a means of managing pain. Exploration of the structure and supports needed to engage patients in creating their song. Allen, 2014		
Songwriting with adults in cardiac care or needing surgical and procedural support.	Considerations and suggested adaptations in utilizing songwriting with medically fragile and critically ill adults.	Heiderscheit, 2014b; Leist, 2014
Songwriting with adults living with HIV/AIDS. Structural and organizational considerations to facilitate engagement and exploration of the client's life. Keith, 2014; Hatcher, 2007		
Songwriting with children with developmental disabilities or behavioral and interpersonal problems.	Exploration of ways to adapt and structure the songwriting experience to support engagement for children with developmental, behavioral, or interpersonal considerations.	McCarrick, 2014; Sokira, 2014

Songwriting during pre-loss children and adults in palliative care.	Descriptions of how the songwriting process can unfold and be utilized to create a legacy project.	O'Callaghan, 2013
Songwriting as a means of communication and expression for 12-year-old diagnosed with ASD.	Illustration of how the MT provides musical choices in the composition process and how this helps to facilitate the client's verbal expression communication and development of song lyrics.	Carpente & LaGasse, 2015
Songwriting with mothers of preterm infants in the neonatal intensive care unit (NICU).	Description of songwriting process during kangaroo care and outcomes from quantitative data and analysis of qualitative data of the songwriting experience with parent–infant dyads	Ettenberger & Beltrán Ardila, 2018
Songwriting with deaf clients dually diagnosed.	Multiple case illustrations implementing songwriting with deaf clients and the way the MT structured the process based on the unique needs of each client.	Ward, 2016
Creating hip-hop songs in pediatric rehabilitation.	In-depth case detailing the therapeutic process of writing the lyrics and music for multiple hip-hop songs with an 11-year-old boy with an acquired spinal cord injury.	Viega, 2015

Other Literature Related to Songwriting with Individuals

The body of research literature has grown significantly in recent years, providing a broader scope of how songwriting is being utilized in music therapy practice. Baker and Wigram (2005) include clinical case examples of songwriting by MTs in many different clinical settings around the world. The authors utilize these case examples to examine the different protocols implemented to structure the songwriting process, themes of the songs, the techniques they used to foster the creation of the lyrics and music, and the function of the song for the clients. Aasgaard and Blichfeldt Ærø (2016) explore developments in the use of songwriting in music therapy practice by reviewing the literature. They include general protocols and guidelines for the songwriting process and integrate clinical examples to illustrate these. They also explore techniques for creating the lyrics and music and discuss how to integrate technology into the songwriting process. This includes identifying various resources and tools that may support the client's process and allow the client to create a recording of their song. The authors also discuss the "afterlife" of songs and the significant role a song can play in a client's life long after the songwriting process is completed.

Baker (2015) provides a comprehensive examination of therapeutic songwriting that includes exploring the factors that influence the process and various songwriting methods and models, as well as limitations and contraindications. There are numerous clinical case examples and diagrams that illustrate the steps involved in the different methods presented. Song lyrics of original songs created by clients are also included to further help elucidate the songwriting method. These provide numerous examples of how the MT can structure and adapt the songwriting experience to foster maximum engagement and to address various therapeutic needs. Recent publications also explore factors that may impact the songwriting process, such as sociocultural (Baker, 2013a) and environmental conditions (Baker, 2013b), which are important considerations when considering songwriting as a therapeutic experience and planning for the session as well.

Songwriting is also being utilized to address many different therapeutic needs. Hatcher (2007) details the songwriting process in addressing the effects of PTSD on an adult living with HIV/AIDS and recovering from addiction, exploring the emotions expressed and evoked in the songs, the meaning they held, and the role they played in helping him to integrate back into society. Tamplin et al. (2016) developed and tested a songwriting protocol for clients who have acquired brain or spinal cord injury. Details are provided about one client who created three songs over the course of 12 music therapy sessions. The songs focus on six domains associated with self-concept: the physical, personal, social, family, academic/work, and moral. The process of writing the songs engages the client in reflecting on their perception of the past, present, and future self. Creating the songs provides them with the opportunity to integrate components of the past self with the present injured self. In this process, songwriting serves as the medium that supports a change in the client's self-concept. Baker and Macdonald (2017) explore the use of songwriting as a means of exploring or re-authoring one's identity and examine this through case literature from different clinical settings. Mantie-Kozlowski et al. (2020) implemented different songwriting method-variations to support and foster conversation strategies for a 64-year-old woman with diminished expressive communication skills due to struggling with logopenic progressive aphasia. Her conversation repair increased from 20% to 80% during the opportunities in songwriting, and she reported it was easier to communicate and that she felt more confident in her ability to communicate as a result.

Finally, the *Guidelines for Music Therapy Practice* series contains information about the selection and design of songwriting for individuals in relation to numerous populations and treatment settings. Some of these chapters are noted in the literature table above, but most chapters throughout the entire series have information on songwriting that may help you to think about why you might select this method-variation for your client and how to best prepare the experience in relation to their specific needs.

Summary

Songwriting can be tailored to meet a myriad of therapeutic needs for clients in many different clinical settings. To support a client's successful engagement in songwriting, it is important that you understand what adaptations are needed and take the necessary steps in designing, planning, and preparing for implementation. Taking time to prepare for the session and organize materials ensures you have what is needed to support the client's engagement in the process. The case studies in the literature on the use of songwriting with individual clients provide considerations, protocols, and recommendations for addressing a wide array of therapeutic needs. This body of research and clinical evidence also helps to illustrate how you can adapt any aspect of the songwriting process to the skills, abilities, needs, and music preferences of clients across the life span.

References

Aasgaard, T., & Blichfeldt Ærø, S. (2016). Songwriting techniques in music therapy practice. In J. Edwards (Ed.), *The Oxford Handbook of Music Therapy* (pp. 644–668). Oxford University Press.

Abbott, E. (2014). Elderly residents in nursing facilities. In L. Eyre (Ed.), *Guidelines for music therapy practice in mental health* (pp. 685–717). Barcelona Publishers.

Allen, J. (2014). Pain management with adults. In J. Allen (Ed.), *Guidelines for music therapy practice in adult medical care* (pp. 36–61). Barcelona Publishers.

Baker, F. (2013a). An investigation of sociocultural factors impacting the therapeutic songwriting process. *Nordic Journal of Music Therapy, 23*(2), 123–151. doi.org/10.1080/08098131.2013.783094

Baker, F. (2013b). The environmental conditions that support or constrain the therapeutic songwriting process. *The Arts in Psychotherapy, 40*(1), 230–238. doi.org/10.1016/j.aip.2013.02.001

Baker, F. (2015). *Therapeutic songwriting: Developments in theory, methods, and practice.* Palgrave Macmillan.

Baker, F., Kennelly, J., & Tamplin, J. (2005). Songwriting to explore identity change and sense of self-concept following a traumatic brain injury. In F. Baker & T. Wigram (Eds.), *Songwriting: Methods, techniques, and clinical applications for music therapy clinicians, educators, and students* (pp. 116–133). Jessica Kingsley Publishers.

Baker, F., & Krout, R. (2009). Songwriting via Skype: An online music therapy intervention to enhance social skills in an adolescent diagnosed with Asperger's Syndrome. *British Journal of Music Therapy, 23*(2), 3–14.

Baker, F., & MacDonald, R. (2017). Re-authoring the self: Therapeutic songwriting in identity work. In R. MacDonald, D. J. Hargreaves, & D. Miell (Eds.), *Handbook of musical identities* (pp. 436–452). Oxford University Press.

Baker, F., & Wigram, T. (2005). *Songwriting: Methods, techniques, and clinical applications for music therapy clinicians, educators, and students.* Jessica Kingsley Publishers.

Bradt, J., Biondo, J., & Vaudreuil, R. (2019). Songs created by military service members in music therapy: A retrospective analysis. *The Arts in Psychotherapy, 62,* 19–27.

Brooks, D. (2014). Professional burnout. In L. Eyre (Ed.), *Guidelines for music therapy practice in mental health* (pp. 767–796). Barcelona Publishers.

Beuchel, T. (2018). Songwriting with a transgender youth undergoing cancer treatment. In A. Heiderscheit & N. Jackson (Eds.), *Introduction to music therapy practice* (pp. 194–195). Barcelona Publishers.

Carpente, J., & LaGasse, B. (2015). Music therapy for children with autism spectrum disorder. In B. Wheeler (Ed.), *Music therapy handbook* (pp. 290–301). Guilford Press.

Christy, J. (2017). *A case study of clinical songwriting in music therapy to address emotional expression among an individual with Parkinson's disease and their family caregivers.* Master's thesis, Radford University, Radford, Virginia. http://wagner.radford.edu/id/eprint/359

Clements-Cortés, A. (2014). Adults in palliative and hospice care. In J. Allen (Ed.), *Guidelines for music therapy practice in adult medical care* (pp. 295–346). Barcelona Publishers.

Curtis, S. (2014). Women survivors of abuse and developmental trauma. In L. Eyre (Ed.), *Guidelines for music therapy practice in mental health* (pp. 263–288). Barcelona Publishers.

Doak, B. (2014). Children and adolescents with emotional and behavioral disorders in an inpatient psychiatric setting. In L. Eyre (Ed.), *Guidelines for music therapy practice in mental health* (pp. 168–204). Barcelona Publishers.

Dun, B. (2014). Children with cancer. In J. Bradt (Ed.), *Guidelines for music therapy practice in pediatric care* (pp. 290–323). Barcelona Publishers.

Dwyer, O. (2007). Would you like to write your own song? Songwriting to address the paradox of emerging capabilities and diminishing possibilities experienced by an adolescent boy with Muscular Dystrophy. *Voices: A World*

Forum for Music Therapy, 7(2). doi.org/10.15845/voices.v7i2.494.

Edgar, J., Tsiris, G., & Rickson, D. (2019) "The screams crashed into silence": A therapeutic songwriting project for young adults with life-shortening illnesses. In A. Ludwig (Ed.), *Music therapy in children and young people's palliative care* (pp. 159–173). Jessica Kingsley Publishers.

Ettenberger, M., & Beltrán Ardila, Y. (2018). Music therapy songwriting with mothers of preterm babies in the Neonatal Intensive Care Unit (NICU). *The Arts in Psychotherapy, 58,* 42–52. doi.org/10.1016/j.aip.2018.03.001

Gardstrom, S. (2014. Adjudicated adolescents. In L. Eyre (Ed.), *Guidelines for music therapy practice in mental health* (pp. 622–657). Barcelona Publishers.

Hatcher, J. (2007). Therapeutic songwriting and complex trauma. *Canadian Journal of Music Therapy, 13*(2), 115–131.

Hatcher, J. (2014). Adult male survivors of abuse and developmental trauma. In L. Eyre (Ed.), *Guidelines for music therapy practice in mental health* (pp. 289–312). Barcelona Publishers.

Heiderscheit, A. (2014a). Spiritual practices. In L. Eyre (Ed.), *Guidelines for music therapy practice in mental health* (pp. 873–910). Barcelona Publishers.

Heiderscheit, A. (2014b). Surgical and procedural supports for adults. In J. Allen (Ed.), *Guidelines for music therapy practice in adult medical care* (pp. 17–34). Barcelona Publishers.

Heiderscheit, A. (2018a). Song composition following trauma. In A. Heiderscheit & N. Jackson, *Introduction to music therapy practice* (pp. 155–159). Barcelona Publishers.

Heiderscheit, A. (2018b). Composition to cope with auto-islet total pancreatectomy transplant. In A. Heiderscheit & N. Jackson, *Introduction to music therapy practice* (pp. 183–185). Barcelona Publishers.

Hilliard, R., & Justice, J. (2011). Songs of faith in end-of-life care. In A. Meadows (Ed.), *Developments in music therapy* (pp. 582–594). Barcelona Publishers.

Jackson, N. (2014). Adults with depression and/or anxiety. In L. Eyre (Ed.), *Guidelines for music therapy practice in mental health* (pp. 339–377). Barcelona Publishers.

Jackson, N. (2018). Songwriting with a young boy with anger issues. In A. Heiderscheit & N. Jackson, *Introduction to music therapy practice* (pp. 192–194). Barcelona Publishers.

Johnson, E., & Rickson, D. (2018). Songwriting with adolescents who have mental health difficulties: One music therapy student's experience. *New Zealand Journal of Music Therapy, 16,* 115–137.

Keith, D. (2014). Adults with HIV/AIDS. In J. Allen (Ed.), *Guidelines for music therapy practice in adult medical care* (pp. 237–264). Barcelona Publishers.

Kennelly, J. (2014). Brain injuries and rehabilitation in children. In J. Bradt (Ed.), *Guidelines for music therapy practice in pediatric care* (pp. 356–402). Barcelona Publishers.

Kim, S. (2014). Stress reduction and wellness. In L. Eyre (Ed.), *Guidelines for music therapy practice in mental health* (pp. 797–839). Barcelona Publishers.

Kooij, C. (2009). Recovery themes in songs written by adults living with serious mental illness. *Canadian Journal of Music Therapy, 15*(1), 37–58.

Lewis, J. (2019). *The experience of songwriting in music therapy for adults with intellectual disability.* Master's thesis, Molloy College, Rockville Centre, New York. ProQuest Dissertations Publishing, 27542969.

Lindberg, K. (1995). Songs of healing: Songwriting with an abused adolescent. *Music Therapy, 13*(1), 93–108.

Mantie-Kozlowski, A., Mantie, R., & Keller, C. (2020). Therapeutic songwriting as a meaningful relationship-oriented activity to establish communicative opportunities during therapy for an individual with PPA. *Aphasiology.* doi:10.1080/02687038.2020.1812248

Marin, M. (2014). Exploring therapeutic songwriting for Filipino children with leukemia. *Music & Medicine, 6*(1), 17–24.

McCarrick, P. (2014). Behavioral and interpersonal problems in school children. In M. Hintz (Ed.), *Guidelines for music therapy practice in developmental health* (pp. 193–232). Barcelona Publishers.

Melendez, K. (2014). Adult females in correctional facilities. In L. Eyre (Ed.), *Guidelines for music therapy practice in mental health* (pp. 559–621). Barcelona Publishers.

Mondanaro, J. (2014). Surgical and procedural support for children. In J. Bradt (Ed.), *Guidelines for music therapy practice in pediatric care* (pp. 205–251). Barcelona Publishers.

Murphy, K. (2014). Adults with substance use disorders. In L. Eyre (Ed.), *Guidelines for music therapy practice in mental health* (pp. 449–501). Barcelona Publishers.

Neugebauer, C. (2014). Children in general inpatient care. In J. Bradt (Ed.), *Guidelines for music therapy practice in pediatric care* (pp. 477–512). Barcelona Publishers.

O'Callaghan, C. (2013). Music therapy preloss care through legacy creation. *Progress in Palliative Care, 21*(2), 78–82. doi:10.1179/1743291X12Y.78 0000000044

Roddy, C., Tamplin, J., Rickard, N., & Baker, F. (2018). Exploring self-concept, well-being, and distress in therapeutic songwriting in participants following acquired brain injury: A case series analysis. *Neuropsychological Rehabilitation.* doi.org/10.1080/09602011.2018.1448288.

Rogers, P. (2014). Children and adolescents with PTSD and survivors of abuse and neglect. *Guidelines for music therapy practice in mental health* (pp. 313–338). Barcelona Publishers.

Rolvsjord, R. (2005). Collaborations on songwriting with clients with mental health problems. In F. Baker & T. Wigram (Eds.), *Songwriting: methods, techniques, and clinical applications for music therapy clinicians, educators, and students* (pp. 97–115). Jessica Kingsley Publishers.

Sokira, J. (2014). Rett Syndrome. In M. Hintz (Ed.), *Guidelines for music therapy practice in developmental health* (pp. 87–107). Barcelona Publishers.

Street, A. (2012). Combining functional and psychoanalytic techniques, using rhythmic auditory stimulation (RAS) and songwriting to treat a man with a traumatic brain injury. *Voices: A World Forum for Music Therapy, 12*(3). https://doi.org/10.15845/voices.v12i3.673

Tamplin, J., Baker, F., Macdonald, R., Roddy, C., & Rickard, N. (2016). A theoretical framework and therapeutic songwriting protocol to promote integration of self-concept in people with acquired neurological injuries. *Nordic Journal of Music Therapy, 25*(2), 111–133. doi: 10.1080/08098131.2015.1011208

Tileston, P. (2014). Adults and adolescents with eating disorders. In L. Eyre (Ed.), *Guidelines for music therapy practice in mental health* (pp. 402–448). Barcelona Publishers.

Vega, V. (2014). Adults with traumatic brain injury. In J. Allen (Ed.), *Guidelines for music therapy practice in adult medical care* (pp. 145–177). Barcelona Publishers.

Viega, M. (2015). Working with the negatives to make a better picture: Creating hip-hop songs in pediatric rehabilitation. In C. Dileo (Ed.), *Advanced practice in medical music therapy: Case reports* (pp. 46–60). Jeffrey Books/Music Therapy Resources.

Ward, A. (2016). Music therapy interventions for deaf clients with dual diagnosis. *Voices: A World Forum for Music Therapy*, *16*(3). https://doi.org/10.15845/voices.v16i3.840

Zanders, M. (2014). *Foster care youth.* In L. Eyre (Ed.), *Guidelines for music therapy practice in mental health* (pp. 205–236). Barcelona Publishers.

6

SONGWRITING WITH GROUPS

Group songwriting is a music experience in which a group of clients compose an original song or any part of the song (e.g., lyrics, melody, accompaniment) (Bruscia, 2014; Heiderscheit & Jackson, 2018). In the group songwriting process, clients will need and use varying levels of technical support from you, the MT, depending on their skills and abilities. Group songwriting is similar to songwriting for individuals (discussed in Chapter 4) in that the clients may create song lyrics and/or the melody for their song, compose the accompaniment, or notate their song. The primary difference is that you have a group of clients engaged in creating the song and making decisions as a collective group throughout the process. The process of creating a song as a group provides an opportunity to explore and discover how to co-create a song and to collaborate throughout the process. The song they create collectively can then become an artifact representing their shared experiences as well as their collaborative process. The group song can be utilized to review their therapeutic process and progress, serve as a record or reminder of their process, or be shared with others to communicate their experiences or therapeutic experiences.

Prerequisites

There are some prerequisites to consider when you are exploring the option of engaging a group in a songwriting experience. Much like songwriting with an individual, the songwriting process with a group can be tailored, adapted, and structured in ways to meet the varied skills, strengths, and limitations of the group. Understanding each individual in the group and how they engage as a group will allow you to plan and prepare for each session and ensure you have the tools and resources in place to support the songwriting experience. A prerequisite is that the clients must have receptive language skills to understand the directions you give the group. The clients must be able to make decisions and to work with others to make decisions as a group. The clients also need to have some expressive language to be able to communicate their thoughts and ideas with the group.

Risks and Contraindications

There are inherent risks when engaging a group of clients in a collective and unfamiliar task. For a group to engage effectively in a shared experience such as songwriting, they need to have established a sense of cohesion as a group to be able to make decisions and work together to create their song. This will require the group to listen to each other, communicate with each other, compromise and make decisions together, and be respectful of differing ideas.

Songwriting can often be a new and unfamiliar experience for an individual and even less familiar as a collective or group experience. Clients may feel apprehensive and vulnerable about engaging in a new and unfamiliar experience and feel an uneasiness about participating in this process with a group. Clients who have difficulty in communicating and expressing their ideas, thoughts, and emotions may feel uncomfortable in sharing these with the group, as well as in having these included as a part of a song.

Many of these risks can be managed and minimized through careful planning and adapting the structure of the experience to the capabilities, skills, and therapeutic needs of the group. Understanding the group's level of cohesion and development as a group can help you be aware of these potential risks, recognize when challenges may arise in the group process, and respond within the session to minimize any disruption to the experience.

Group songwriting experiences are contraindicated for clients who are not orientated to reality to the extent that this interferes with the effective use of language and communication skills. It is also contraindicated when group members are not able to listen to each other; do not feel safe in sharing their thoughts, feelings, or ideas with the group; or are unable to work together to make decisions.

Affordances and Challenges

There are many different affordances inherent in the group songwriting experience. There are also many aspects of the group songwriting experience that may serve to challenge a group in ways that support their therapeutic growth and development. The decision to select songwriting as a method and how you adapt and structure the process for the group provide affordances that may be unique for the group, as well as challenges that can be adapted to accommodate the members' preferences, strengths, skills, abilities, and needs. While there are several affordances and challenges specific to the group songwriting experience, it is important to understand that you can tailor and adapt the process to provide unique affordances and challenges for your group. This process draws upon your critical thinking, creativity, and music skills to explore how to structure and adapt the process to best meet the therapeutic needs and integrate the skills and abilities of any group.

Group decision-making. Creating and writing a song is a process that requires a group to make many different decisions about the various aspects of the song. These decisions will require the group to discuss and come to a collective agreement about the topic, lyrics, style or genre of the music, form, tonality, instrumentation, and so on. Many clients may not have musical knowledge or musical skills and may need support to be able to make decisions about the music. A group may also have a clear idea of what they want their song or piece to sound like. The group may need to hear examples of rhythms, tonality, instruments, and so forth to help them to make decisions about the music. It is important to empower the group in making these decisions to ensure they feel a sense of ownership of their composition.

Self-organization. The structure and steps inherent in the group songwriting process allow each member of the group to organize their thoughts, feelings, and behaviors. This may include sharing ideas about a song topic and suggestions, words, or phrases for lyrics; listening to others' ideas; responding to what is being shared by others; and/or sharing their thoughts about musical aspects or elements for the song. Clients may be challenged to communicate and listen to each other, stay focused on the task at hand, and/or write about a topic that is personal and meaningful. For group members to feel ownership of their song, they need to recognize that their input is represented in the song and throughout the songwriting process.

Group problem-solving. The process of creating a song as a group will be new and unfamiliar for many clients. They may feel anxious as they engage in an unfamiliar experience, as they do not know what to expect or what they may be asked to do. This provides clients with the opportunity to explore how they manage this discomfort and not allow their fears or concerns to interfere with their engagement. The process of writing a song as a group may challenge a group in how to make decisions related to any aspect of the song (topic, lyric, genre, instrumentation, etc.); this challenge can provide them with an opportunity to explore possible solutions and determine the best solution or option for the group.

Self-expression within a group. The songwriting process provides opportunities for clients to share and express their thoughts, feelings, experiences, and ideas, as well as to hear from other members of the group. This mutual sharing can foster a sense of connection to others in the group, validate one's experiences and feel heard, and encourage them to share their feelings. As clients engage in the process of writing lyrics or creating the music, they continue to share their thoughts and ideas to make collective decisions regarding their song or music. While self-expression plays a key role in the songwriting process, it can create feelings of vulnerability for clients as they may feel more vulnerable sharing in a group experience.

Cooperation and conflict resolution. Creating a song as a group is a co-creative process that requires clients to share, listen, be respectful, and make space for one another throughout the process. This process provides opportunities for clients to work together in making decisions, discussing ideas, listening to each other, and working through challenges or disagreements that might arise. You may integrate structures to support this group experience to help foster their cooperative process, or the group may be able to determine their process for collectively working together to create their song.

Trusting others. Engaging in a new group experience provides an opportunity for clients to practice trusting others. Clients also need to have a sense of safety within the group in order to take risks and engage in a new and different experience with others. Clients also need to feel safe and secure in the client–therapist relationship to trust that the therapist would not engage the group in an experience they are not ready to tackle in their therapeutic process.

Collective thematic exploration. Creating a song that is an expression or representation of a group's collective or shared experiences provides opportunities to disclose and share their experiences. Sharing one's experiences allows for reflection, encourages others to share, fosters the development of awareness and insights, and encourages recognition of common experiences. As group members share their own experiences, they may feel a sense of support, reflect more deeply, and learn from the experiences of others in the process. Disclosing and sharing their experiences and discovering commonalities in their experiences also fosters a sense of cohesion, helping to build new connections as a group. Additionally, it may be in discovering these common experiences that the group finds a topic or focus for their song.

Creating a collective message. Composing a song allows a group of clients to create an artifact that expresses and communicates a message that they have worked to co-create. The process of collaborating creates a collective message that provides a means of support for one another and fosters a sense of connection and empowerment. The message expressed in their song may be a reflection of their common or shared experiences, serve as a reminder or anthem for group members as they continue in their respective therapeutic processes, or be a message to share with others to help them to understand the group members' feelings or experiences.

Create an artifact that documents a shared experience or process. Co-creating a song about a group's shared or common experiences allows a group to produce an artifact that captures, communicates, and represents their therapeutic process. This artifact is a representation of this moment in each of their lives, as well as their shared process as a group. If the group decides to make a recording of their song composition, it becomes an artifact they can keep and listen to again and again, reflecting on their therapeutic process and the experience of creating their composition. The group may decide to share their song or music in a live performance or make a recording that can be shared with others. A group's decision to share their creation provides them with the opportunity to allow others to understand their experiences, thoughts, and feelings. They may also feel a sense of empowerment from having others hear their collective message.

Many clients may not have musical knowledge or skills and may need support to make decisions about song structure or music to accompany their song. A group may have a clear idea of what they want their song to be about or what they want it to sound like. Each group is unique, and this can necessitate different levels of structure. It is important to recognize what structures the group needs to engage in the songwriting experience and to support and empower the group in making decisions throughout the process to ensure they feel a sense of ownership of their composition.

Orientations to Clinical Decision-Making

Outcome Orientation

Outcome orientation focuses on the needs of the group. In a group setting, the therapist must consider the overall needs of the individuals who are members of the group and the common needs they may have. These needs may have been identified in their assessment or may emerge in the therapeutic process. If you are working from outcome orientation, you will identify and formulate the specific therapeutic goals that will be addressed in the songwriting experience. Identifying the therapeutic goal(s) for the group can help you to determine specific affordances and challenges inherent in songwriting that can address the group's therapeutic goals. Perhaps the group needs to practice sharing and listening to develop their social or communication skills, or maybe they need to work on making decisions and resolving conflict. In an outcome-oriented approach, group songwriting lends itself to measurable results. Additionally, the nature of the songwriting process and the role of the music in the experience foster change in an objective manner.

Music as agent. In group songwriting, the group and the therapist are working to create an original song as a means of engaging with each other collaboratively to practice working together and completing a shared task. The process requires the group to make collective decisions and choices as they share and discuss their respective ideas. Group members may disagree at times and experience frustration as they work to find solutions. As they work together, they may also foster connections; as a result, music becomes the agent of change, influencing the clients' responses and behaviors during the experience.

Music as skill. Group songwriting is selected to provide opportunities to practice skills; through the process, these skills are developed and transformed. The various aspects of a group songwriting experience deliberately engage these skills that are the focus for development. The skills that are being developed during the group songwriting process are transferable to other situations and contexts outside of music and the music therapy setting. For example, clients need to practice expressing and sharing their thoughts and feelings and listening to others. The group songwriting experience will necessitate that the clients listen to one another and engage in sharing their own experiences. This turn-taking process is needed for the group to determine a topic and create meaningful lyrics and music for their song. Working collaboratively in this process affords them multiple opportunities to practice and develop these skills and meet their treatment goals. They are then able to take these skills outside the therapeutic environment and practice using them, enabling them to engage these skills in different contexts.

Music therapy protocols. The group songwriting process can be utilized as a treatment protocol that is relevant to the therapeutic needs or goals of the group as a whole. The songwriting process may be focused on addressing a general therapeutic need for the group, such as fostering resilience and a sense of empowerment for adults in addictions treatment as they engage in a new and unfamiliar process. This may be accomplished over the course of three sessions, as the group collaborates in creating their song lyrics, works together to compose the melody and accompaniment for their song, and records their song to share with others. This process is focused on nonmusical outcomes and engages the clients in a collaborative music experience that supports their capacity to make these changes in the music therapy process.

Experience Orientation

Experience orientation strategies engage clients in music experiences that provide opportunities for the clients and therapist to clarify and address the group's therapeutic needs. The MT and group begin the music experience with a general understanding of the group's needs, but the therapeutic needs are clarified through the experience as they discover new insights about their therapeutic needs. For example, a group of young adults in eating disorder treatment may compose a song about what it is like to live with an eating disorder. In the process of sharing their experiences and writing their lyrics, they may discover how isolated they are from loved ones and their support systems when they are actively engaged in using eating disorder symptoms. They may recognize that when they are isolated, they are also more vulnerable and likely to have eating disorder symptoms. Discovering this in the process of composing their song can help them to recognize their need to work on connecting to others rather than isolating and how fostering these relationships may be key to their recovery.

Music as process. Group songwriting can provide a music experience to address a basic therapeutic need and allow other needs to emerge in the process. For example, group songwriting may be utilized with a group of women in prison. The MT and group may decide to use songwriting as a way to engage the women in expressing their thoughts and feelings. The group experience provides opportunities for each to communicate their thoughts and feelings and to experience being heard. As the group practices these skills in the songwriting process, they may begin to recognize how vulnerable, affirming, and validating it feels to share their feelings. They may also start to explore and question why they have not been permitted to or felt they could express their feelings and which relationships in their lives have left them feeling 'silenced.' Through this experience, they may develop insights about codependent and dysfunctional relationships that have led them to believe that their feelings, thoughts, and experiences do not matter. As they gain this new awareness, the therapeutic process can be modified and adapted to address this need that has emerged.

Music as representation. The group songwriting process can result in the creation of a musical product if the group decides to create an artifact of their song. This can take the form of a printed copy of their composition, a recording, or a performance of their song. This product is a reflection of their collective experience of creating their song, as well as a representation of how they have been transformed as a part of this experience. The group may listen to their recording and reflect on their experience of co-creating the song. Each group member may also be given a recording to have. Group members may listen to their recording long after it was created and reflect on their therapeutic journey, or they may share it with friends or loved ones to help them to understand their therapeutic process and how they have changed.

General Considerations and Procedural Guidelines

When you have determined that songwriting is the music experience that can best address the therapeutic needs and goals of the clients participating in the group, you will need to focus on planning the session, including ways to support engaging the clients, observe their responses in the experience, explore and determine how you need to adapt the process for the clients, understand how you can support the process as their song creation unfolds, work with the group to determine how they want their song accompanied and whether they want to be involved in playing the accompaniment, and finally, bring the session to a close. This process will require you to think creatively as you strive to structure and adapt the experience in ways that allow each member of the group to engage in the songwriting process. There are many ways to adapt the group songwriting process to make it accessible to clients with various skills and abilities.

Planning: In planning the songwriting experience for your group, you need to understand the specific skills, abilities, and limitations of each group member, as well as their ability to communicate and work collaboratively as a group. This may include any of the following:

- Language and communication skills (verbal and nonverbal)
- Cognitive abilities (concrete or abstract thinking)
- Ability to attend to and listen to each other (how long can they focus)
- Ability to express and communicate their feelings
- Ability to work together and cooperate
- Ability to compromise
- Ability to share thoughts and ideas with others
- Ability to recall and share their experiences
- Ability to recognize common or shared experiences
- Group members' music preferences
- Musical skills and knowledge that group members possess

When you have a clear understanding of the group's overall skills, abilities, and limitations, you can then determine the level of structure that you will need to foster their engagement in the collaborative songwriting process.

- Do you need specific tools or resources to support communication in the process, such as pictures, communication devices, paper, and writing utensils to communicate ideas for themes or lyrics?

- Can the group collaborate to identify a topic or theme for their song, or do you need to come in with ideas to share with the group and have them choose?
- Can all of the clients communicate or share their ideas with the group to ensure they are a part of the group process?
- Can all of the clients read, or will they need to learn the lyrics by rote to make a recording?
- What genres of music do members of the group prefer?
- What instruments or equipment are needed to accommodate these music preferences?
- Do any of the clients play an instrument that they may want to incorporate into the song?
- Are there instruments the clients prefer or are able to play for their song?

These questions will help you to understand and determine what materials and instruments you will need for the group songwriting process and to record or perform the song.

- Communication tools (pictures, photos, devices, etc.)
- Paper or writing utensils to allow clients to write down their ideas
- White board or large paper to write down themes and lyric ideas that are visible for all members of the group
- Instruments
- Electronic equipment or apps to produce beats or rhythms
- Laptop or tablet with software to create an audio recording
- Camera to make a video recording
- Microphone

The materials you use may be dependent upon your clinical setting or what is available to you. If you are limited due to restrictions in your clinical environment or due to budget, think creatively about how you might utilize free resources or apps that may be available to use. The clients may have ideas and resources to suggest as well, so this could be something you discuss with the group. A group needs to understand that they cannot record the group song on their personal mobile devices, as this would be a privacy and HIPAA violation.

Engaging. The directions you provide to the group will help them to understand the process and foster their engagement. As you understand the structure needed, this will help you to determine, based on the cognitive-developmental level of the group members, the instructions you need to give to the group and how you need to present them. You may even consider whether it is helpful to have the directions or an overview of the process written down for the group.

- Describe the songwriting experience to the group, share the purpose or intention for choosing this method-variation, and tell them what they will be asked to do in the process.
- Facilitate a discussion with the group to brainstorm and identify a topic or theme for their song
- When the topic or theme has been determined, facilitate a discussion to share words or phrases for the lyrics.
- Write these ideas on a white board or large piece of paper so everyone can see them.
- After the group has shared words and phrases, it is helpful to discuss the structure of the song and to help the group to determine whether there are specific words or phrases they want to be repeated in their chorus.
- Depending on the ideas that are shared for the lyrics, the group may create a verse or the chorus first.
- Ideas about the melody or rhythm of lyrics may evolve as the group is creating their lyrics.
- Sing through each verse as they are completed and discuss with the group any changes they want to make.
- When the song is written, sing through it again to see if there are any changes the group wants to make.
- If the group began the process by writing the lyrics, the next step is to create the music to accompany their song. Keep in mind that group songwriting can begin by writing the music and then the lyrics. Refer to Table 4.0, as the process will be the same for the group.

- Discuss with the group what sounds they imagine as they think about their song. Consider the genre or musical style, tonality, rhythm, instrumentation, and so forth. The lyrics may provide hints to feelings or moods being communicated. It may be helpful for the group to hear examples of these to be able to make a collaborative decision.
- The decisions the group makes about the melody and/or accompaniment may help to determine instrumentation for their song; if they are stuck, then the next step would be to discuss with the group the instrumentation they would like.
- If there are members of the group who play an instrument, you may want to provide the opportunity to have them play a part of the accompaniment if possible.
- When all of the musical decisions have been made, play and sing through the song with the group and discuss whether there are any changes they want to make.
- The group can decide whether they want to make a recording of their song.
- If the group decides to record their song, you will need to know how you can provide a recording of their song that is HIPAA-compliant. See Chapter 12 for more information about this.

Observing. In the group songwriting process, it is important to observe how group members are engaging, how they are listening, and how they are responding to each other. You may need to provide prompting to engage the group in generating and sharing ideas. You will need to facilitate the discussion to ensure that each group member can share their input.

- Is the group able to share their ideas for a theme or topic?
- Does each member of the group feel invested in or have a meaningful connection to the theme or topic?
- Is the group able to identify topics that relate to them as a group?
- Are group members able to listen to each other?
- Are group members able to respond to the ideas that others share?

- Is the group able to engage in making a collective decision?
- Is the group able to manage difficulties or disagreements they experience in the process?
- How are group members responding to each other in the process?
- Is every member of the group engaging in the process?
- Does the group need prompting or support to explore and discuss their own experiences and feelings to foster their engagement?
- How are the group members reacting to what they are creating?
- Do members of the group have the skills and abilities to contribute to the song musically?
- Do members of the group have an interest in contributing to the song musically but need support to do so?
- Is the group able to listen to each other to play and sing their song?

Adapting. The support and assistance a group will need in the songwriting process will depend on several factors: their skills, abilities, cohesiveness as a group, and music experiences. Many clients have not engaged in songwriting; as a result, group songwriting may be an unfamiliar experience. The group's ability to work together is dependent on their interpersonal skills and their formulation as a group. If the group encounters difficulty in engaging in discussion and listening to each other or making decisions, you may need to provide prompts or structures to foster their engagement.

The way the group can engage in making musical decisions and playing an instrument as a part of the accompaniment will also be dependent on previous music experiences. Group members may be eager to contribute musically but need structure and adaptions to make this feasible. This can require you to think creatively about how to make instruments accessible. This may include color-coding notation, integrating rhythm-based instruments with rhythm patterns tailored for the group, playing the guitar in an open tuning, and so on. Creating these musical opportunities for members of the group allows them to take greater ownership of their song and bolster their connection as a group and their sense of accomplishment.

The group may decide that they want to create a recording of their song. It will be important to discuss with the group whether everyone wants to be on the recording. When decisions about recording their song have been made, the group can proceed with rehearsing and determining whether changes need to be made. Writing and recording a song as a group may need to occur over multiple sessions. It will be important to be aware of the time the group needs and to communicate this so they know what to expect.

Developing. Group songwriting is a multistep, dynamic, and complex process. You are striving to engage multiple clients in a shared process. Group members are likely engaging in a new experience, sharing their ideas, and may develop new insights as they create their songs. The structure, support, and prompting you provide will help the group to generate and develop their ideas. Discussions of these ideas can create opportunities for the group to explore topics or their feelings more deeply and to develop new insights. Engaging the group in this collaborative experience may also foster a new sense of self for members of the group. Working together on this shared task may further develop their group cohesion. It will be important to ask questions that facilitate sharing ideas, clarifying what they share, as well as to process and explore what group members are disclosing. This will help the group to further develop their ideas and support generating new understandings. The process of co-creating a song can be a significant accomplishment, validating what they can do together

The group will need to make music decisions for their song. Members of the group may or may not have musical knowledge or skills, and this will impact how you structure this part of the process and support the group in making decisions. If there are limitations or constraints on the instruments available for their song, it will be important to inform the group about what options are available to them. You may need to provide musical examples and samples of sounds to develop their understanding of these musical elements and to be able to make informed decisions as a group.

Members of the group may wish to sing their song or to play an instrument to accompany their song. The song belongs to the group, and decisions about performing and recording their song need to be made collectively. It will be helpful to discuss the options with the group based on their expressed interests:

- Clients sing and play the accompaniment.
- Clients sing and play accompaniment with musical support from you.
- Some clients sing and some clients play accompaniment.
- Clients sing and you play accompaniment.
- Clients sing the song a cappella.
- Clients sing the melody while you sing harmony or backup vocals.
- Clients sing the melody, record harmony, record accompaniment, and tracks are mixed.

The musical choices need to be made by the group. What they want for their song and what musical elements will help to express and communicate the message embodied in their song. Explore and discuss how these different musical elements help to communicate the intention of their song, as this can foster a deeper understanding of the meaning of their song. Additionally, engaging the group in these decisions also helps them to recognize and acknowledge that they were able to accomplish something they had not done before.

Accompanying. Group members will need to discuss what role they each play in singing, performing, and/or recording their song. Regardless of how active or passive the role that each group member chooses to play, it is important to provide them with options for engagement based on their level of comfort. You want to ensure that you do not overtake the process by making decisions but instead empower the group to make their own choices. This will also be important when it comes to accompanying the group. You can play examples of accompanying patterns and let them choose. You can provide support in the accompaniment that supports their ability to sing together or play the accompaniment. It will be important to ask the group in this process of developing the accompaniment whether the music captures the sound they wanted for their song and, if not, what changes they would want to make.

Reviewing. When the group has completed writing the lyrics and music and has had the chance to sing or record their song, it is important to reflect and review their process. Hearing, singing, and playing their song in its entirety allows them to take in their completed product. The questions you ask the group will be tailored to their process, their unique experience, and the level to which they can reflect on and process their experience.

- What was it like to work together to co-create a song?
- How did you feel after hearing your song?
- How did you feel about working together in the process?
- How did it feel to sing, perform, and/or record your song?
- What did you enjoy about the process?
- What was challenging about the process?
- Is there anything you discovered or learned in the songwriting process that may relate to your life?
- What meaning does this song hold for you?
- Is there anything you would like others to understand or learn from your song?

Responses to the questions you ask may foster disclosures from other members of the group. You may also have follow-up or clarifying questions as well. Remember that while a song is a product, the process of creating it is a therapeutic experience. It is important to allow this time of reviewing and reflection to maximize the therapeutic experience.

Closing. The songwriting process may occur over more than one group session. If this is the case, you need to consider how you will close each session until the process is completed. For example, you may only be able to get the lyrics created in the first session and you will focus on composing the music in the next session. At the end of the first session, you will want to take time to review what the group was able to do and their experience of that part of the process. When they have reflected on their experience, you can then talk with the group about what you will work on in the next session. You will continue this process until the entire process is completed.

If the group chooses to make a recording of their song, they now have an artifact of what they created, their experience of co-creating their song, and their therapeutic process. The recording created needs to comply with HIPAA regulations and protect everyone's privacy; this needs to be communicated to the group, along with how the recording will be made available to them. It will be valuable to have the group listen to their completed recording and to allow them to respond to their song. The group may choose to share what they learned from the experience. You can validate what you witnessed as they engaged in the process. This is an opportunity for you to validate their ability to work together in the therapeutic process.

Special Considerations

Group songwriting with children. In general, children have not developed the capacity for abstract thinking, and this will impact how you structure and plan the group songwriting experience. You will need to be sure to provide clear and concrete directions, using terms and concepts appropriate for their developmental understanding. You will need to consider the group's ability to express and communicate their own, feelings, thoughts, and ideas. You may need to provide the group with opportunities to choose words or phrases to fill in the blanks rather than to construct full phrases for song lyrics. They may have limited reading and writing skills, which may require using visual aids to assist in creating their song and helping them to learn their song by rote. Their ability to listen and communicate with one another in a group is an important consideration in group songwriting. You may need to provide structure to ensure that every member of the group has the opportunity to contribute and share their input. The group may need support to ensure that they listen to each other, consider each other's ideas, and make decisions together. Children do not have nuanced interpersonal skills, so you will need to embed the structure and support to help them to practice these skills. It is also important to keep in mind that children's vocal range is limited. Melodies that move in a stepwise fashion will be most appropriate rather than having large leaps in the melody line.

You will need to use musical terms that children understand when composing the music for their song. If the group members want to accompany their song, you will want to ensure that the rhythms are simple enough for them to play, that they can play with minimal instruction, and that they can play cohesively as a group.

Group songwriting with adolescents. Creating a safe space and structure is an important consideration for adolescents who struggle with self-acceptance and have concerns about being judged or rejected by others as they struggle with forming their own identity. This can be challenging in a group where one's intersectionality, as well as that of their peers, increases their awareness and sensitivity of differences (such as gender identity and expression, socioeconomic status, cultural identity, race, and religion). This can also apply to differences in music preferences. It will be important to provide clear expectations about safety and being respectful of each other's thoughts, feelings, and experiences. The group may be able to take an active role in identifying and determining these expectations, which can give them ownership and great accountability to each other. You can validate this by modeling these behaviors and demonstrating these expectations through your actions as you facilitate. It is important to engage everyone in the process and to not move ahead without ensuring that everyone's feelings, thoughts, and ideas have been expressed and that what they as a group want to be integrated into their song has been collectively agreed upon. This will help everyone to feel they have been valued in the process of creating the lyrics and music for their song.

Group songwriting with adults. These considerations will be dependent on the unique skills, abilities, and needs of the group. It is important to recognize and have an overall understanding of the group's interpersonal skills and how well they can listen and communicate with one another. You can provide directions and structure to create a safe space, to foster their sharing, and to help them to understand that everyone's input is welcomed and valued. There may be diverse music genre preferences, so it can be important to consider that these music elements of different genres can be integrated to create a fusion of styles.

Group songwriting with older adults. Older adults may have sensory deficits or other physical challenges that may impact their ability to engage in the group songwriting process. They may have difficulty with hearing, sight, memory, and motor skills. It is important to understand the sensory capabilities of the group members, as this will inform how you plan, structure, and adapt the process. Your group may have very good communication skills, but they may have difficulty in reading and writing. You may consider writing in a large font on a white board in a dark marker and ensuring that everyone is seated close enough to see it. It will be important that the group members are seated close enough to each other to hear one another, as well. Hearing loss in upper registers is common in older adults, and the vocal range often becomes smaller as well. You may need to sing in a lower range and avoid very large leaps in the melody. Clients may need to sing or accompany their song at a slightly slower tempo. You may also need to adapt instruments or mallets that allow them to grip or hold to play.

References

Bruscia, K. (2014). *Defining music therapy* (3rd ed.). Barcelona Publishers.

Heiderscheit, A., & Jackson, N. (2018). *Introduction to music therapy practice.* Barcelona Publishers.

7

GROUP SONGWRITING — ILLUSTRATIONS AND EXAMPLES IN THE LITERATURE

Group songwriting requires the MT to understand the skills, abilities, needs, and dynamics of the group and to utilize this knowledge in planning, designing, and implementing this method-variation. The case illustration included at the start of this chapter provides an example of the considerations that an MT explores when designing and planning a session and the reflexive nature of the therapeutic process when facilitating a group songwriting experience. The review of the literature included in this chapter offers additional case examples that demonstrate the myriad ways in which the MT can structure the songwriting experience to meet the therapeutic needs of a group by making use of the opportunities and challenges available in this method-variation. The chapter also includes an overview table of group songwriting case examples, with a brief description of each case and a summary of the focus of the songwriting experience, along with the reference in case you want to read the full clinical case. Last, there is a brief review of the literature that highlights group songwriting research and resources.

Group Songwriting with Adolescents in Inpatient Mental Health Treatment

The group of eight adolescents ranged in age from 15 to 17 years old and were admitted to an inpatient mental health unit due to recent suicidal and homicidal thoughts, as well as drug and alcohol use. Two of the adolescents had been transferred to the unit from a medical unit due to severe alcohol poisoning and a drug overdose. In the previous music therapy session, they had engaged in a song discussion. In the process of talking about their thoughts and feelings related to the song, members of the group began to share ideas about how words of the song could be changed and how this could alter the meaning of the song and better represent their own experiences. The MT recognized the group's interest in tailoring a song as an expression of their unique experiences and, as a result, shared with the group how they could transform a song or create an original song. The group asked questions about both method-variations and discussed with the MT what they would need to do and that they would like to choose the style or genre of music for their song. The MT assured them that the song could be in the style of their preferred genre. The group discussed these options, as well as their ability to write an original song. Their discussion indicated a desire to create an original song, but they doubted their abilities. The MT asked if they felt there were genres of music they preferred that also felt more accessible to them. The group immediately talked about how they liked to rap and hip hop, with their friends and some would often make up their lyrics and rap and hip hop songs spontaneously. Discussing these options and their preferred music styles and genres helped the group to decide they wanted to create an original song in rap form.

In the music therapy session the next day, the MT asked them to share their ideas for a topic for their song, keeping in mind that the topics needed to connect to each member of the group. The MT wrote each idea on a white board and asked the group to examine the ideas to see if these topics were connected in any way. This prompted the group to identify several topics they felt were related. These topics included using drugs and alcohol, feeling out of control, suicidal and homicidal thoughts, and understanding the impact of drugs and alcohol. The MT asked the group whether these were the topics that they wanted to use as the focus of their song. When they agreed, all other topics were erased from the board. The MT then asked the group questions about each of these topics to help to clarify their thoughts and ideas and generate ideas for lyrics. The MT discovered in this process that one member of the group did not feel that he had experienced any negative impact from using drugs and alcohol. The other members of the group shared the negative experiences they had had as a result of using drugs and alcohol, such as feeling depressed and suicidal, missing school, and getting angry and violent. The MT asked the group members how using drugs and alcohol had contributed to these thoughts, feelings, and behaviors. They were able to identify that drinking and using left them feeling tired, unmotivated, skipping school, or not doing homework, which led to feeling depressed and not caring about life. The MT asked the group questions to support and guide their discussion, which helped them to identify and explore the negative effects of drugs and alcohol. This discussion helped one member of the group to begin to examine and understand that his admission to the unit was not someone's fault but a decision his parents made to keep him safe because he was engaging in dangerous behaviors due to his drug use and drinking as well as threatening to harm others.

This discussion helped the group to reach a consensus on how to approach their song. The MT was then able to ask questions to guide the songwriting process. The group decided to focus the song on how their alcohol and drug use had started and then focus on the negative impacts that it had had on in their lives. The MT asked the group what they were doing in treatment that was helping them to make changes. These questions provided the structure and support that the group needed to work collaboratively to create the lyrics to their song. When the group was satisfied with their lyrics, the MT asked each member (who wanted to) to select a rap beat on the drum machine and share it with the group. The group listened to each rhythm. The MT asked them to consider each beat and, as they listened, to consider how the beat would support the message of their song. The group discussed their thoughts about each beat and was torn between two different beats. To help their decision-making process, the group rapped their lyrics with each beat. This helped them to determine which of the two beats felt like the right fit. The lyrics to their song titled "I'm Your New god" are included here:

> *Curiosity got me involved in this thing I'm in*
> *Now I sit alone with my bottle of gin*

Hallucinations they take over my mind
Realizing now that drugs were never kind

I realize now that I was to blame
I'm your new god, you can call me cocaine
Addictive, violent, crazy indeed
To be on top of the world, yeah that's what I need

Drugs led me to believe that people should die
Having fatal thoughts of suicide
Thinking every day about doing the job
So, I went back and talked to my god

I talked and I talked 'til I finally got through
I realize now what drugs can do
I feel all-powerful and can't be changed
Now I'm happy that my life's rearranged

I realize now that I was to blame
I'm your new god, you can call me cocaine
Addictive, violent, crazy indeed
To be on top of the world, yeah that's what I need

We've worked real hard to learn what not to do
We all know now what drugs and alcohol do
We want to live life even when it gets tough
We know that we all have to talk about stuff

I realize now that I was to blame
I'm your new god, you can call me cocaine
Addictive, violent, crazy indeed
To be on top of the world, yeah that's what I need

The group decided they wanted to make a recording of their song. They divided up the verses and sang the chorus together. They felt that singing the chorus together would serve as a reminder of how they worked together, even long after treatment. They thought that whenever they listened to their rap, they would remember the support of the group, how they worked together to create their song, and how the song served as motivation to continue to work hard to stay sober. In Chapter 12, you will read about the group's process of recording their song and the technology utilized to capture their recording.

Literature Illustrating Songwriting with Groups

MTs adapt the structure of a method-variation and their way of facilitating the composition process to address the needs and to support the engagement of the group. This section examines three clinical cases of group songwriting, exploring the decisions that the MT makes in planning, designing, implementing, and facilitating group songwriting experiences. These clinical cases also illustrate how the decisions the MT makes to provide structure support the group members' engagement and their process of working together collaboratively. The process is further supported by the MT responding reflexively throughout the experience.

Heiderscheit (2018) describes the process of songwriting with a group of adults who were dually diagnosed with a substance use disorder and mental illness and were attending a day treatment program. The weekly group music therapy sessions integrated a wide variety of music experiences, including receptive, re-creative, and improvisational methods. During a recent receptive music experience in a previous session, group members had identified lyrics that were meaningful to each of them and discussed in detail how the song connected to their experiences. The group was forthcoming in describing their own experiences and demonstrated a vulnerability in this process, which led the MT to explore the idea of song composition with the group. Creating a song could serve as a way to explore their experiences even more, and it could serve as a container for these moments in their lives. Creating an artifact (song) about their experiences could be a reminder of these struggles they had encountered with drugs and alcohol and be a tool to support their recovery. Additionally, it was evident to the MT that the group had a strong level of cohesion based on how they were able to share and engage in discussion with one another. When the idea of writing a song was introduced to the group, they quickly determined that they wanted to create one.

The MT initiated the process by engaging the group in a discussion about potential topics or themes for their song. The group members shared their ideas and listened to each other; as they shared their own experiences and feelings, they recognized commonalities in their experiences. This led the group to identify similarities in the negative experiences they had each encountered due to their addiction. The MT asked the group if this might be a topic for their song. The group felt they could write about this as a topic and that everyone would be able to contribute since they all had experienced the negative impact of addiction. The group was able to focus on bringing their experiences into their song lyrics as they described in more detail their struggles with denial, cravings, feeling powerless, recognizing how much they had hurt their loved ones, the shame associated with their use, and watching their using friends die due to their addiction. The discussion gave them the space in which to talk about their experiences, which became the material of their song lyrics.

When their lyrics were completed, the MT shifted the discussion to what feelings their lyrics communicated. Identifying the feelings represented in the lyrics provided the foundation for identifying the musical genres and styles the group wanted to use for their song. The group identified that their lyrics represented hitting rock bottom and feeling down and out and that there was still a sense of trying to keep going. This helped the group to determine that blues was a genre that would help to best express the essence of their song. The MT was also aware that two members of the group played instruments, and they were invited to contribute to the musical accompaniment. The blues genre also provided the musical structure for each of them to play their guitar and harmonica, as well as space within the composition to vamp within the song structure.

The group recorded their song "Chronic Craving," and each was given a CD of it. When the group listened to the recording, they shared that their metaphoric lyrics served as reminders of how much their addiction had destroyed and disrupted their lives and that it served as a reminder to stay focused on sobriety. Hearing them all sing it together also helped them to remember that they were not alone on this journey of recovery and that their song could provide support after they all left treatment.

This case highlights how the MT shapes and guides the process by asking the group questions, holding the space for them to share their experiences, and helping the group connect their experiences to support the group arriving at a topic for their song. This is carried into the process of making choices about the music. The MT asked questions about the feelings that related to their song in order to empower the group to make decisions about the musical elements. This ensured that the feelings that related to the experiences included in the lyrics were also infused in their musical accompaniment and that the group worked collaboratively to make all of the musical decisions about their song as well.

Edgar, Tsiris, and Rickson (2019) detail a group of three young men in their early 20s who were all living with Duchenne Muscular Dystrophy (DMD), a rare genetic disease characterized by rapidly decreasing muscle weakness that is a life-shortening condition. They each utilized a motorized wheelchair due to their limited mobility. These three young men named their group "The DMDs," and they met 2 hours every week over the course of 12 weeks. The song composition process was initiated after group members had explored their musical identities by sharing and discussing songs and determining how their musical identities could connect and come together to create a shared composition. Each was an experienced gamer with education and experience in information technology (IT). Based on these interests and skills, the MT began their composition process by experimenting with sounds, beats, and loops. The MT also supported the group by exploring various sounds and elements of music that matched their musical identities. The clients also played different excerpts from songs they liked to help the MT to hear and understand what they wanted for their song. The MT supported this creative exchange of ideas to help the group members listen and respond to each other and to negotiate and make decisions for their song. The creative process and development of their instrument tracks fostered their engagement and momentum, and they gained confidence in experimenting with new ideas. This required each to listen to the other members to maintain their creative identity within the song that was emerging. The more invested they became in the process; the more time they needed to discuss and make their collaborative decisions.

While all three indicated they did not want to sing, they did feel that their composition would benefit from lyric content. Reflecting on early sessions, they shared songs that had inspired each of them. These songs and artists served as a starting point, as they identified and selected lyrics and used them as their own. These lyrics were projected on a wall in the group room to foster their discussion of the relevance and significance of each for use in their song. Their lyric content centered on the shared challenges that they all face in living with DMD. The selected lyrics focused on themes of defiance, anger, and fear. They personalized the lyrics with pronouns (I, we, me, us) to reflect their group identity in their song and co-created words that provided an accurate and honest reflection of the challenges they were facing in their lives.

This case illustration highlights the decisions and choices an MT can make based on the skills, knowledge, and interests of the clients. Engaging and supporting the clients in making collaborative decisions throughout the song composition process fostered a sense of empowerment for this group of clients who were challenged day-to-day by the degenerative nature of the disease. The MT structured the process by having each client share music and songs that expressed their musical identity. This discussion revealed shared connections and developed their cohesion as a group and their investment in collaborating in a creative process. This process of co-creating fostered a sense of understanding, as well as of accomplishment for these three young men facing similar acute challenges.

Baker et al. (2018) detail the group songwriting process designed for family caregivers of people living with dementia to share their journeys as caregivers, foster support and connections, and develop inner strength and personal growth. Caregivers participated in six 1-hour sessions, each dedicated to one aspect of the song composition process. The MT utilized the first session to allow each group member to introduce themselves, share their story, build rapport, and foster trust within the group. Sessions 2 through 5 were focused on the creation of the song, including the lyrics and music. Having four sessions dedicated to creating the lyrics and music for their song provided sufficient time for group members to share and listen to each other as they engaged in a creative process together. These sessions were cyclical in nature and included group members sharing their individual stories, finding commonalities in their experiences, and working to shape and craft lyrics that helped to tell their "collective story."

This process included the group sharing their experiences, brainstorming ideas, finding common aspects in their experiences, and then using this content to create phrases or lyrics. It allowed group members to share the struggles they experienced as caregivers, such as feeling forgotten by friends and experiencing loneliness as a result. They also recognized they were finding a sense of connection with each other as they shared their experiences with one another. They used these experiences to co-create their song lyrics, and the chorus they wrote reflected the overall message of their song. While the MT held the primary responsibility for creating the music for their song, group members were engaged in identifying their musical preferences, suggesting musical styles, and making musical choices regarding the melody, harmony, and accompaniment patterns and style. In session six, the group focused on making final changes, refining elements of their song, rehearsing, and, finally, creating their recording.

The group songwriting process provided the opportunity for caregivers to share their experiences, feel heard by others, reflect on their relationship with their loved ones, identify and express positive feelings, and practice releasing negative feelings. This process also helped them to address and manage stress, identify and resolve barriers that interfered with their ability to cope, and work to reframe their experiences and feel validated. Engaging in creating a song as a group helped to combat their sense of loneliness and to connect with others who understood and shared their experiences. Additionally, engaging in this process while their loved ones were in programming gave the caregivers much-needed time and space to tend to their own needs.

These cases provide a window into the group songwriting process and the various ways in which an MT designs and facilitates the process based on the needs, skills, abilities, and interests of the group. There is a wide array of clinical accounts in the literature that describe and explicate the songwriting process with groups in different clinical settings. Table 7.0 includes examples of group songwriting with various client groups that you may wish to explore. A brief description of each case is included, along with details about the focus of the case and also the reference, so you can read the article or chapter if you choose.

Table 7.0

Case Examples of Group Songwriting in the Literature

Description of Case	Focus of Case	Reference
Use of songwriting as a means of orientation with older adults with dementia	Exploration and descriptions of various ways to structure and facilitate the songwriting process with clients with dementia	Hong & Choi, 2011
Group songwriting to develop coping skills and working alliances with clients in addiction treatment and to manage cravings in detox	Procedure for the use of songwriting as a psychoeducational tool to assist clients in developing coping skills	Silverman, 2012, 2019
Guidelines for structuring and facilitating group songwriting with older adults	Suggested procedures for designing, facilitating, and adapting the songwriting process	Abbott, 2014
Ways to address professional burnout through group songwriting	Guidelines for structuring and facilitating the group songwriting process to foster group engagement	Brookes, 2014
Different functions of songwriting in clients' therapeutic processes (e.g., assessment, observation, treatment) with children and adolescents in mental health treatment	Suggestions for structuring and facilitating group songwriting process to accommodate the developmental and psychosocial needs of the group	Doak, 2014
Adapting the structure of group songwriting for adults in mental health treatment	Guidelines for facilitating the process to support group engagement; suggestions and alternatives for adapting the process to address group needs	Eyre, 2014a, 2014b
Procedures for group songwriting with adjudicated adolescents	Guidelines for designing, structuring, facilitating, and adapting the songwriting process	Gardstrom, 2014

Functions of group songwriting to address spiritual needs of clients	Descriptions of various therapeutic needs and goals that group songwriting can address	Heiderscheit, 2014
Different ways to structure song composition processes for adults dealing with depression and anxiety	Guidelines and suggestions for designing, facilitating, and adapting the song composition process	Jackson, 2014
Considerations for designing and facilitating the song composition experience for stress reduction and wellness	Suggestions for various adaptations of the song composition process	Kim, 2014
Exploration of the therapeutic implications of group song composition for incarcerated adult women	Considerations when designing and facilitating detailed information in writing the lyrics and creating the music	Melendez, 2014
Considerations for designing and facilitating song composition with juvenile male sex offenders	Suggestions and adaptations to support and foster group engagement and collaboration in the composition process	Rea-Kolb, 2014
Structuring and adapting the group song composition process for clients with Alzheimer's and other dementias	Suggestions for creating consistency needed for clients with dementia to support their engagement in the song composition process	Young, 2014
Group songwriting with individuals who have experienced various types of trauma	Brief case vignette describing the group process of creating and recording their song, with song lyrics included	Borczon, 2014, 2015
Song composition with clients in addictions treatment	Therapeutic goals and processes that song composition addresses and excerpt of song lyrics created by clients	Murphy, 2014, 2015
Use of songwriting with a client in eating disorder	The different roles of the composition process and the	Tileston, 2014; Trondalen, 2016

treatment	role of the song in the client's treatment process	
Use of songwriting with asylum seekers and refugees	Process of songwriting to address trauma, social isolation, and stress of relocation and acculturation	Harrison, Jacobsen, & Sunderland, 2019
Use of songwriting to address mental health and well-being in university students	Description of the process of structuring the songwriting process and suggestions for prompts to address well-being and mental health needs of university students	Gee, Hawes, & Cox, 2019
Songwriting with children experiencing homelessness and family violence	Exploration of the collaborative nature of the songwriting process with children experiencing trauma	Fairchild & McFerran, 2019
Songwriting protocol designed for adolescent bereavement	An eight-session songwriting protocol designed to connect protective factors of self-esteem, coping emotional expression, and meaning-making in adolescent bereavement	Myers-Coffman et al., 2020

Other Literature Related to Songwriting with Groups

Clinical case illustrations are valuable resources for understanding how song composition is structured and facilitated by MTs with different client groups, as well as for helping us to understand what informs an MT's clinical decision-making throughout the composition process. Another valuable resource is the book *Therapeutic Songwriting: Developments in Theory, Methods, and Practice* (Baker, 2015). There is a chapter in this book dedicated to group songwriting that explores how the process is shaped by the personalities of group members, considerations for the size of groups, developing group cohesion, navigating group conflict, and the implications of open and closed groups.

While the body of literature surrounding song composition with individuals is substantial, the literature exploring the effect and impact of group songwriting has been growing in recent years. Myers-Coffman et al. (2019) examined the effect of an eight-session group songwriting program with adolescents grieving a loss. Participants reported feeling a sense of togetherness in the sessions, with songwriting as a safe way to express emotions related to their grief. The program gave them a way to strengthen their coping skills. The study findings indicate that this collaborative songwriting process may help to decrease levels of grief, provide social support, and enhance creative expression. Garcia-Valverdi et al. (2020) explored the effect of group songwriting on the quality of life of caregivers of loved ones with dementia. Participants attended 12 weekly 1-hour sessions. Sessions 1 through 4 were designed to develop group cohesion by utilizing receptive, re-creative, and improvisational methods to prepare the group for the songwriting process. Sessions 5 through 7 utilized singing and music collage to engage the group in identifying topics that were meaningful to them, as well as transforming phrases and words. This process helped the group identify the topic of their song. Sessions 8 and 9 engaged participants in creating the lyrics for their song, as they discussed and reviewed words, metaphors, and phrases to use in the verses and chorus. Session 10 focused on creating the music; the participants discussed the melody, harmony, rhythms, and music genre for their song. Based on their choices, the MT provided the harmonic base on which the group could create their melody. In sessions 11 and 12, the group made decisions about instrumentation and recording for their songs. Songs were shared in the final session as a means of closure. The results from the study indicate that group songwriting decreased anxiety and depression and increase self-esteem and quality of life.

Clark et al. (2021) examined the use of therapeutic songwriting (TSW) in spousal and family dyads with individuals living with dementia and their caregivers. Groups of four to six members each were formulated based on dyad locations and relationships. The TSW program was composed of six weekly 1-hour sessions. Participants indicated that TSW was a positive shared experience that benefited caregivers and individuals living with dementia and fostered further engagement with music. The creative process stimulated mental processes, reconnected participants to interests, and highlighted existing skills and abilities. TSW provided opportunities to reflect, recall memories, and reminisce about life experiences. The collaborative nature of group songwriting prompted interactions and led to greater social connection, experiences of inclusion, and feelings of empathy.

Gibbons-Hogan et al. (2020) examined over 100 songs written by 110 clients engaged in inpatient mental health treatment group music therapy sessions. Song themes focused on topics of love, spirituality, and the meaning of life and illness. Interviews with 11 clients identified themes related to the process of writing and collaborating, expressing emotions, the benefit of using music during hospitalization, and the relationship between their mental illness and music. McCaffery et al. (2021) also explored the impact of group songwriting with mental health service users. The clients participated in three songwriting group sessions and composed three songs during these sessions. Their song lyrics reflected themes about growth, feeling a sense of empowerment, freedom, and empathy for others in the songwriting process. Focus group interviews with participants following the sessions revealed that they felt that group songwriting helped them to break down barriers, offered them new perspectives, and helped them to explore perceived vulnerabilities and discover how music can promote well-being. Overall, group songwriting provides "a meaningful, reciprocal and equitable space" (p. 41) that fostered a co-creative experience that aligned with a recovery-orientated mind-set.

Finally, the *Guidelines for Music Therapy Practice* series, as mentioned in previous chapters, is recommended to you as a resource for further developing your understanding of selecting, designing, and implementing songwriting for groups while taking into consideration the characteristics of these groups from a diagnostic or population perspective. Most chapters throughout the series include information about songwriting.

Summary

Group song composition is a creative and collaborative process that can address many different therapeutic needs. MTs design, structure, facilitate, and adapt the process to address the unique needs, skills, abilities, and interests of the group. The literature on group songwriting provides many different examples of how MTs adapt the process to engage the group in creating the lyrics, music, and recording of their composition. This literature also demonstrates how MTs can make song composition accessible to groups of clients. The research literature surrounding group song composition method-variations indicates how different types of clients and caregivers benefit from the creative therapeutic group experience. Clients and caregivers consistently indicate that the group song composition process fosters a sense of connection, creating a safe place for expression. As the body of research regarding group songwriting and its therapeutic benefits continues to grow, this will foster the exploration of this method-variation in new and different clinical settings, producing new findings to further inform our practice.

References

Abbott, E. (2014). Elderly residents in nursing facilities. In L. Eyre (Ed.), *Guidelines for music therapy practice in mental health* (pp. 685–717). Barcelona Publishers.

Baker, F. (2015). *Therapeutic songwriting: Developments in theory, methods, and practice.* Palgrave Macmillan.

Baker, F., Stretton-Smith, P., Clark, I., Tamplin, J., & Lee, Y. (2018). A group therapeutic songwriting intervention for family caregivers of people living with dementia: A feasibility study with thematic analysis. *Frontiers in Medicine, 5,* 151. doi:10.3389/fmed.2018.00151

Borczon, R. (2014). Survivors of catastrophic event trauma. In L. Eyre (Ed.), *Guidelines for music therapy practice in mental health* (pp. 237–262). Barcelona Publishers.

Borczon, R. (2015). Music therapy for survivors of traumatic events. In B. Wheeler (Ed.), *Music therapy handbook* (pp. 390–400). Guilford Press.

Brooks, D. (2014). Professional burnout. In L. Eyre (Ed.), *Guidelines for music therapy practice in mental health* (pp. 767–796). Barcelona Publishers.

Clark, I., Baker, F., Tamplin, J., Lee, Y. E., Cotton, A., & Stretton-Smith, P. (2021). "Doing things together is what it's about": An interpretative phenomenological analysis of the experience of group therapeutic songwriting from the perspectives of people with dementia and their family caregivers. *Frontiers in Psychology, 12,* 598979. doi:10.3389/fpsyg.2021.598979

Curtis, S. (2014). Women survivors of abuse and developmental trauma. In L. Eyre (Ed.), *Guidelines for music therapy practice in mental health* (pp. 263–288). Barcelona Publishers.

Doak, B. (2014). Children and adolescents with emotional and behavioral disorders in an inpatient psychiatric setting. In L. Eyre (Ed.), *Guidelines for music therapy practice in mental health* (pp. 168–204). Barcelona Publishers.

Edgar, J., Tsiris, G., & Rickson, D. (2019). The screams crashed into silence: A therapeutic songwriting project for young adults with life-shortening illnesses In A. Ludwig (Ed.), *Music therapy in children and young people's palliative care* (pp. 159–173). Jessica Kingsley Publishers.

Eyre, L. (2014a). Adult groups in the inpatient setting. In L. Eyre (Ed.), *Guidelines for music therapy practice in mental health* (pp. 69–114). Barcelona Publishers.

Eyre, L. (2014b). Adults in recovery model setting. In L. Eyre (Ed.), *Guidelines for music therapy practice in mental health* (pp. 115–167). Barcelona Publishers.

Fairchild, R., & McFerran, K. S. (2019). "Music is everything": Using collaborative group songwriting as an arts-based method with children experiencing homelessness and family violence. *Nordic Journal of Music Therapy, 28,* 88–107. https://doi.org/10.1080/08098131.2018.1509106.

Garcia-Valverdi, E., Badia, M., Orgaz, M., & Gonzalez-Ingelmo, E. (2020). The influence of songwriting on the quality of life of family caregivers of people with dementia: An exploratory study. *Nordic Journal of Music Therapy, 29*(1), 4–19. doi:10.1080/08098131.2019.1630666

Gee, K., Hawes, V., & Cox, N. (2019). Blue notes: Using songwriting to improve student mental health and well-being. A pilot randomized controlled trial. *Frontiers in Psychology, 10*(423). doi:10.3389/fpsyg.2019.00423

Harrison, K., Jacobsen, K., & Sunderland, N. (2019). New skies above: Sense-bound and place-based songwriting as a trauma response for asylum seekers and refugees. *Journal of Applied Arts and Health, 10*(2), 147–167. doi:10.1386/jaah.10.2.147_1

Heiderscheit, A. (2014). Spiritual practices. In L. Eyre (Ed.), *Guidelines for music Therapy practice in mental health* (pp. 873–910). Barcelona Publishers.

Heiderscheit, A. (2018). Song composition with a group in dual diagnosis treatment. In A. Heiderscheit & N. Jackson, *Introduction to music therapy practice* (pp. 149–152). Barcelona Publishers.

Hogan-Gibbons, C., Short, A., & Isobel, S. (2020). Mental health inpatient experiences of songwriting: A qualitative study. *Australian Journal of Music Therapy.* Advance online publication. Retrieved from https://www.austmta.org.au/journal/article/mental-health-inpatient-experiences-song-writingqualitative-study

Hong, I., & Choi, M. (2011). Songwriting-oriented activities improve the cognitive functions of the aged with dementia. *The Arts in Psychotherapy, 38,* 221–228. doi:10.1016/j.aip.2011.07.002.

Jackson, N. (2014). Adults with depression and/or anxiety. In L. Eyre (Ed.), *Guidelines for music therapy practice in mental health* (pp. 339–377). Barcelona Publishers.

Kim, S. (2014). Stress reduction and wellness. In L. Eyre (Ed.), *Guidelines for music therapy practice in mental health* (pp. 797–839). Barcelona Publishers.

McCaffrey, T., Higgins, P., Monahan, C., Moloney, S., Nelligan, S., Clancy, A., & Cheung, P. (2021). Exploring the role and impact of group songwriting with multiple stakeholders in recovery-oriented mental health services, *Nordic Journal of Music Therapy, 30*(1), 41–60. doi:10.1080/08098131.2020.1771755

Murphy, K. (2014). Adults with substance use disorders. In L. Eyre (Ed.), *Guidelines for music therapy practice in mental health* (pp. 449–501). Barcelona Publishers.

Murphy, K. (2015). Music therapy in addictions treatment. In B. Wheeler (Ed.), *Music therapy handbook* (pp. 354–366). Guilford Press.

Myers-Coffman, K., Baker, F., & Bradt, J. (2020). The resilience songwriting program: A working theoretical model and intervention for adolescent bereavement. *Nordic Journal of*

Music Therapy, 29(2), 132–149. doi:10.1080/08098131.2019.1642373

Myers-Coffman, K., Baker, F., Daly, B., Palisano, R., & Bradt, J. (2019). The resilience songwriting program for adolescent bereavement: A mixed methods exploratory study. *Journal of Music Therapy, 56*(4), 348–380. https://doi.org/10.1093/jmt/thz011

Scrine, E. (2019). "It's like mixing paint": Songwriting alternative gender cultures with young people as an "after queer" methodology. *Voices: A world forum for music therapy, 19*(3). https://doi.org/10.15845/voices.v19i3.285.

Silverman, M. (2019). Effects of group-based educational songwriting on craving in patients on a detoxification unit: A cluster-randomized effectiveness study. *Psychology of Music, 47*(2), 241–254. doi:10.1177/0305735617743103

Silverman, M. J. (2012). Effects of group songwriting on motivation and readiness for treatment on patients in detoxification: A randomized wait-list effectiveness study. *Journal of Music Therapy, 49,* 414–429.

Tileston, P. (2014). Adults and adolescents with eating disorders. In L. Eyre (Ed.), *Guidelines for music therapy practice in mental health* (pp. 402–448). Barcelona Publishers.

Trondalen, G. (2016). Expressive and receptive music therapy in eating disorder treatment, In A. Heiderscheit (Ed.), *Creative arts therapies and clients with eating disorders* (pp. 99–119). Jessica Kingsley Publishers.

8

INSTRUMENTAL COMPOSITION

In instrumental composition, the client composes a piece of music that might consist of melody, harmony, rhythms, or any combination of these, which can then be performed on instruments. Instrumental composition may involve the development and/or use of adapted or original notational systems that make it possible for clients without a musical background to actively participate in a compositional process. Likewise, instrumentation for a composition may range from traditional orchestral instruments to physically adapted instruments to specialized instruments (e.g., choir chimes, Orff instruments) to electronic instruments and might even include voice. Note that in the case of using voice as an instrument, we are specifically referring to vocalization that does not include any use of language. These various choices in instrumentation and notation are what make instrumental composition a feasible option for clients of a wider range of ability than you might initially think. It is an excellent option in your music experience "menu" for clients for whom music composition experiences that center on language are therapeutically less useful. Instrumental composition experiences result in a score of some kind from which the music can be re-created, and the process can easily transition into other method-variations with a performance of the composition that may occur live or a recording of the composition that is made for future listening.

Prerequisites

Clients must possess cognitive capabilities for decision-making and communication of preferences in order to participate in a compositional process. Since it is they who are driving the composition, the creative decisions need to be led by the client and not by the MT. Even in cases in which you are providing musical options for the client, it is the client who must make the decisions that lead to the final musical result if they are going to benefit from the affordances of a compositional process. Clients need not be verbal to actively participate in composition, but they must have the ability to understand language to the extent to which they can understand the purpose of the experience and can respond to directives that assist and focus their active participation. In some cases, capabilities that allow them to recognize and respond to symbols may also be a necessity if they are going to use or assist with the development of notational systems.

If the clients are going to use the instruments themselves during the composing, they must be able to physically manage them. Instrument choices for the client should be matched with their physical capabilities. For example, if a preschooler is going to use a drum in the compositional process, you must be able to provide drums that match the physical stature and strength of the child. Traditional djembes and conga drums would not be useful in this type of instance because a young child would not be able to manage them effectively.

Risks and Contraindications

Instrumental compositional processes may be overwhelming for some clients, particularly those who have no musical experience or training, much like a blank piece of paper might be for the individual without previous experience in drawing or writing. This can lead to feelings of frustration or anger, or it might impact the client's sense of competence and self-efficacy. If the client feels as though the demands of the experience are more than they have the resources to meet, they may shut down and refuse to participate or may simply stop coming to sessions. To increase their success, you can mitigate all of these risks with careful consideration of the balance of challenge and demand within the experience and with thoughtful preparation of structures and resources tailored to the client's specific needs.

As with all group composition experiences, there is always the risk that some clients may feel left out of the compositional product if their choices and preferences are not included in a recognizable way. There may be stronger group members who assume too much control in the creative process and who favor certain choices or disallow the musical expressions of other group members. Conflict may also arise between group members in making choices about the composition. You must consider the likelihood of these situations within the group and be prepared to provide structure that allows all clients to actively participate and to hear themselves reflected in the final product. If the group has not developed enough cohesion to allow a group decision-making process to be successful, then instrumental composition may be contraindicated at this time. You might then choose other method-variations that can help to build group cohesion and then return to the instrumental composition choice at some time in the future as the group's needs indicate.

Instrumental compositional processes are contraindicated for clients in states of low consciousness and for those with severe cognitive limitations. Those who are experiencing a psychotic break may not be able to focus on the task at hand long enough to reasonably make decisions for the completion of a composition. You will need to consider whether you can keep the client physically active in the compositional process for enough of the session time for them to remain reality-based and focused; if you cannot, then instrumental composition is contraindicated for that client. Likewise, individuals who are in cognitive decline, such as some with dementia, may not be able to attend to the task over time to complete a composition that maintains meaning and relevance for them. If this is the case, another method-variation may be the better option.

Affordances and Challenges

Nonverbal self-expression. The limits of language may hinder the ability of some clients to express themselves, either because of their lack of language command or because their thoughts and feelings are more complex than can be described in language. At other times, feelings must be expressed before they can be recognized and given a name. Instrumental composition may be a choice that can afford the client the means of expressing themselves without the need to label, explain, or in some other way elaborate using language. The product of instrumental composition can be re-created as many times as desired so that the expression can be relived or further examined through other musical means.

Self-organization. In contrast, nonverbal self-expression lacks the structure of language on which some clients might rely as a means of avoiding full emotional awareness and expression. Instrumental composition affords the client a means of organizing their thoughts and feelings without the limiting structure of language and challenges them to develop musical ways of expressing themselves that do not rely on predetermined structures. In order to do this, the client must determine and shape the structures within the sounds and the overall structure of the composition that reflect the expressive content. Alternately, the client may select a pre-existing compositional structure (e.g., a blues progression or rondo form) and then must organize original musical content within this structure to create an expression that communicates their intent.

Decision-making. As with all compositional method-variations, decision-making is a highly useful affordance of composing instrumental pieces. Along with the more concrete skills involved in making choices (e.g., which instrument? which harmony?), instrumental composition allows clients to sharpen their self-awareness and identify the most precise ways of expressing and communicating thoughts and feelings. Without the use of language, the client must rely solely on their decisions about the sound of their music and how this can be translated into a notated form. As an example, consider a client who is improvising instrumentally. They can freely allow their thoughts and feelings to flow into the sounds and music that they are extemporaneously creating. In order to make this an instrumental composition, however, they must decide exactly which sounds, melodies, harmonies, and rhythms are the best to express these thoughts and feelings and exactly which organization of these elements is most accurate so that they can be notated into a score.

Cooperation and conflict resolution. In group work as well, instrumental composition removes some of the structure that might typically ease the process of creating together, namely language. This may afford the group who is composing together the chance to develop more finely tuned social skills, particularly in practicing interactive listening skills and developing the capacity to accept individual differences. While it may be a challenge for some clients to agree on ideas that are language-based, agreeing on meaning and expression that is being translated into instrumental sound and music increases the challenge to the group members to more clearly express themselves to each other and to be more open to creative ideas that may not match their own.

Orientations to Clinical Decision-Making

Outcome Orientation

Instrumental composition tends to be somewhat of a process-oriented experience, but it may still be useful from an outcome orientation in a number of ways, particularly because of interactional behaviors that are integral to composing, as well as due to concrete aspects of composition such as the notational systems that may be used.

Music as agent. Instrumental composition may be a useful means of working on learning and memory skills when notational systems are a focus of the compositional process. If a color or symbol notation system is developed with a client or group, the use of this system to create the score of a composition will require the clients to understand and remember the system, both in working to put elements of the composition together and then in re-creating what has been composed to adjust it for the final product. For example, if a group has developed a color system to notate a piece they want to write for choir chimes, they need to match the color notation to that of the instruments, translate the sound they want from the instruments onto a score, and, if the score has multiple lines for different players, follow their line of the score to play what they have composed. To make any changes, they will need to identify the part of the score they want to change and renotate it to represent the desired sound.

Music as skill. Instrumental improvisation can be useful if nonmusical behaviors are the target of treatment. Any number of social skills might be addressed if the composition is made within a group setting, including turn-taking, sharing, respectful interactions, appropriate self-expression, frustration tolerance, and so forth. In this case, the composition process itself is merely a tool for the practice of the identified skills.

Music therapy protocols. It is possible that in a particular client's situation, the MT may be able to outline a treatment protocol that identifies defined goals and objectives that are met within an established time period and that utilizes an instrumental composition method-variation. However, in general, this method-variation may not be the best choice if nonmusical outcomes are the intended target of treatment. Strict adherence to a timed plan for an intended outcome is likely to conflict with the creative process needed to compose a meaningful product that is as abstract as an instrumental composition.

Experience Orientation

Instrumental composition lends itself quite well to an experience orientation because composing is a process in and of itself. When composing, the client is making musical choices related to therapeutic material; trying them out; shaping, altering, or replacing them with other choices; and developing musical ideas. This is creative problem-solving in which each decision is made in relation to the previous one and changing one aspect may lead to changes in other aspects of the composition as well.

Music as process. Instrumental composition involves the development of musical ideas, so it is process by nature. Therapeutically speaking, the process of working with musical ideas opens the door to the exploration of both musical and nonmusical content. Musically, the sounds being created by the client may illicit feelings, emotions, and perhaps even memories.

Regardless of whether these match the beginning intention of the composition, they may become an important aspect of the process that influences how the composition develops, how the final product sounds, and what it means to the client who creates it. Non-musically, the problem-solving involved in composing a piece that sounds a particular way and expresses something about the composer may highlight emotional and behavioral patterns that play a role in the composer's daily life and interpersonal interactions. This awareness that arises from the process provides the chance to work with these patterns and perhaps practice different ways of dealing or coping with situations that instigate the behavioral patterns.

Music as representation. Instrumental compositions lend themselves well to representation because they can be focused on expressing a specific idea or intention in sound. For example, a client may be exploring feelings and emotions around a specific experience in their life that are difficult to convey in language and may use an instrumental composition to give these feelings and emotions a sonic form. Or, for the client who has lost the ability to communicate through language, an instrumental composition can provide an outlet for sharing their inner experience with others. Like songwriting, instrumental compositions may also be created as a gift or legacy for others, in which case the client will focus their instrumental piece on the expression that they want to make to the recipient.

General Considerations and Procedural Guidelines

After you have decided that instrumental composition might be a good choice to offer your client, you must consider several things in advance. First, are there preparatory steps that need to be taken with the client before they will be able to successfully engage in instrumental composition? For example, if you will need to devise a notational system for them, they may need to learn and practice this system prior to being able to use it to compose. Also, you will need to consider what instruments you have at your disposal to offer the client. If you are working with a client with some musical background who plays an instrument, do you have this instrument available for their use? And, if you don't, will they be satisfied in using an alternate instrument? Will they want to orchestrate multiple instruments? If so, do you have access to technology that will assist them in listening to what they are composing to fine tune it? You must also consider how much time an instrumental composition process might take and balance this with the potential needs and wishes of the client. If the client is likely to want to create a complex or extended composition and your session time is limited, it might be wise to consider a different compositional method-variation that can be completed more successfully within the available time.

The general considerations that follow are by no means all potential considerations. They will, however, help you to think about the many aspects involved in designing and implementing instrumental composition experiences. As you gain more experience in designing and implementing this method-variation or as you come to know and understand your client better, you will begin recognizing more specifics that you need to consider within the process.

Planning

- Determine your client's specific abilities and limitations in relation to participating in an instrumental composition experience, including all of the relevant domains of functioning.
    - Concrete or abstract thinking?
    - Reading and writing capability?
    - Able to attend, and for how long?
    - Able to work with others?
    - Musical preferences?
    - Musical experience?
    - Musical knowledge?
    - Technology knowledge and skill?

- Determine the notational system that will be most effective for the client's compositional process and whether they will need to learn or practice using the system prior to beginning with composition.
    - Traditional music notation and staff?

- Altered notation and staff?
- Symbols or colors, with or without staff?
- Electronic program for translating playing into a music score?

• Determine the resources you have on hand to assist the client in composing for an instrument or instrument group, as well as your own level of competency in using these resources.
  - Orchestral instruments that they play?
  - Orchestral instruments that you play?
  - Specialty instruments (e.g., choir chimes, orchestra bells, Orff xylophones, drums, world percussion, etc.)?
  - Electronic instruments or instrument apps (e.g., GarageBand, FL Studio, electronic drum kit, etc.)?

• Consider whether your client will need some sort of adaptive equipment or other adaptive resources, such as special mallets or instrument-stabilizing devices, in order to play the instrument on which they want to compose.

• Consider the client's ability to notate the score and prepare the materials and resources needed to facilitate the notation.
  - Staff paper and pencil that the client uses or that you use?
  - Staff on a white board with markers that the client uses or that you use?
  - Stickers for color or number notation and paper, poster, or board on which to attach them?
  - Modified notational symbols in picture form and a board on which to attach them?
  - Cards, stickers, markers, and or other materials from which a new notation system can be made?

• If your client is using a staff on a white board or an adaptive notation system on a poster or board, prepare the treatment space so that they can move freely between the notational surface and the instrument(s) being used to create the composition.

• Prepare examples of music that might help the client to decide what they want their composition to sound like. Remember that they may choose to compose melody, harmony, rhythm, or any combination thereof, so have music samples that reflect these different elements in combinations that make sense for the abilities of the client.

Engaging

- Describe the general process of instrumental composition to your client or group and work with them to clarify the focus or intent of what they will compose.

- If you are using or devising an adapted notational system, explain notational systems to them and assist them in understanding how to use one for composition.

- If it is a new notational system, explain it and practice using the system until the client or group feels comfortable with the symbols and what they mean.

- If you are developing a system together, give them choices about the type of symbols that they will understand and be able to remember, (e.g., numbers, colors, etc.). Practice using the new system prior to starting the composition.

- For clients who have the cognitive ability to use a legend, make one for the adapted system on a white board, poster, or other large surface that can be displayed to assist clients during the compositional process.

- Assist the client or group in deciding which musical elements will be included in their composition.

- Introduce the instrument and music resources that are at their disposal for composing. Make sure that you limit the choices to those which the client or you can use competently so that their expectations for the final product can be reasonably met.

- Decide what parts of the process the client will take responsibility for and which you will carry out. This, of course, can shift and be adjusted as the compositional process unfolds, but help the client to understand that aspects of the composition for which they do not have the requisite skills (e.g., playing a particular instrument, notating on a traditional music staff) can still be included if they will allow you to actively collaborate with them.

- Limit the working sections of the composition to a length that corresponds to the client's organizational capabilities. Clients with more limitations may need to work on a single phrase, while a client with few limitations and music training may be able to work on an entire section at one time.

- Try out the client's musical ideas as they unfold so that they have a sense of how their musical choices sound and how they fit into a whole.

- Make suggestions from which they can choose if the client seems to be stuck for ideas. Be careful, though, to offer ideas for their choice only and not to take over the decision-making. The composition must reflect the client's expression, not the MT's.

- Add to or adjust the notation with each musical choice the client makes so that all ideas are captured.

- When the client feels the composition is complete, play it through and verify that it sounds the way the client wants it to sound. If it does not, identify and mark in the score the places the client wants changed and then return to exploring these sections to make needed adjustments.

Observing

- Notice how the client problem-solves during the experience and make note of where they demonstrate difficulty or frustration.
    - Is the difficulty or frustration with the completion of the steps of the composition or with the feelings that the compositional process elicits?
    - Is there indication that a trauma response has been triggered?
    - Are they having difficulty in re-creating a sound that they want?

- If composing in a group, are all group members actively engaged or are some feeling left out? Does everyone have a role in the process that meets their capabilities?

- Make note of points in the composition that seem to elicit a stronger response from the client. Is this an area that needs further developing?

- Be attentive to the focus or intent of the composition.
    - Is the client or group keeping this focus in mind while making decisions?
    - Do they need redirection in order to refocus?
    - Has the intent or focus shifted in relation to issues that have come out of the process so far?

- What are the reactions to the overall product as the composition begins to take shape?
    - Is there pride or a sense of accomplishment in the result? Have feelings and emotions come to the surface that need to be addressed?
    In a group, does everyone feel that their contribution can be heard in the final product?

Adapting

- Is the client as actively engaged in the compositional process as they can be? If not, why is this?
    - Were their capabilities in relation to the demands of composition over- or underestimated? And how can the level of challenge be adjusted to increase their engagement?
    - Change the notational system?
    - Increase or decrease the responsibilities of the client?
    - Increase or decrease the complexity of the composition?
    - Do they understand what they are supposed to do and why they are creating the composition?
    - If composing in a group, do they each have a meaningful role to fill in the process?

- If the intent or the focus of a composition has shifted during the process, help the client to re-assess the work they have already completed and how they want the final composition to sound.
    - Does the shift change what has already been composed?
    - Are there instrument changes that the client would like to make?
    - Are there specific music elements that should be removed or added?

Developing

- Return to points in the composition at which you notice a stronger or heightened response from the client. Explore what this response is about and encourage the client to adjust the composition to fully express their thoughts and feelings.

- Encourage the client to actively perform whatever part of their composition they are able to play so that they can feel how it is to actually re-create it as opposed to just listening to it. Explore their thoughts and feelings in this regard.

- At any point in the composition where the client or group is not sure that the sound expresses what they want, assist by providing suggestions for how to musically elaborate.
    - Might elements be added or removed?
    - Is there a melody, a phrase, or a rhythmic pattern that should be expanded or explored further?
    - Is there a section that no longer fits into the whole?

Accompanying

- Assist the client in playing, or play for them, the parts of their composition as they take shape so that they can have a sense of what the whole will be like.

- In the case of this method-variation, you might think of recording the notation as a form of accompaniment. In cases where the client is working competently in musical exploration of their ideas, keeping notation of what they are exploring can help to provide for them the support that they need in making choices and utilizing their explorations in formulating the final piece.

Reviewing

- If the client's compositional process extends over a number of sessions, which would not be uncommon, it is a good idea to review the focus or intent of the composition and what was accomplished in the previous session. This will help the client return to where they were in the process.

- Listen to the full composition together when it is complete. It is desirable to record the client, group, or yourself performing it, as this will allow you to listen multiple times and make notes together if there are parts of the composition that the client would still like to change or reconsider.

- Discuss the client's or group's reaction to the final product.
    - Does it fully express what they intended?
    - What did they learn about themselves in the process?
    - Did the focus of the composition change during the process? If so, what insight did they gain from this shift?
    - What meaning does the final product have for the client or the group?

Closing

- Make a final score of the composition and give it to the client or to each group member. If a recording was made, include it with the score.

- Discuss with the client where and how they might like to share their composition with others outside of music therapy and perhaps outside of treatment. If the composition was intended as a gift or legacy, provide the needed number of scores and/or recordings for sharing.

Special Considerations

With children. The intent of composition for children may involve less introspection and more fostering of feelings in the present moment due to limited abstraction ability. For example, instead of exploring a personal issue, a child's compositional process may support the development of feelings of efficacy and competence or may bolster self-esteem. Or, it might provide a means for a child to sonically describe an internal experience for which they have not yet developed language. Adjust the structure of the composition process to match the developmental level of the child. Shorter compositions that can be completed within a limited time frame may be more reasonable than a compositional process that extends over multiple sessions.

An easily understandable notation system is also a necessity for children. While children are often highly creative, shaping their creative process into something that can have a meaningful form and can be re-created will require careful planning and implementation of needed structures. Predefining things such as phrase length, limited instrumentation, clear notation in a large visual format, and so on can provide the container for children's seemingly boundless imagination and creativity. On the other hand, you should be prepared to be flexible and to add aspects that you may not have thought of in advance, within reason.

Consider how children might share their compositions. Since these products may be a source of great pride for them, encourage them to perform whatever part of the composition that they can in order to share it with others. Practice performing it together so that they have confidence in re-creating it. Provide them with scores that they can read using simplified, adapted notation and give instructions for how they might perform them away from music therapy, such as using a pot or pan as a drum or rice or beans in a container as a shaker for accompaniment.

With older adults. Physical limitations may be an issue for older adults who are participating in instrumental composition. Declines in sight and hearing, as well as systemic physical issues like arthritis or balance problems, may require some special preplanning. Consider adaptive equipment for instruments that might ease grasp or range of motion problems. Ensure that you can set up the environment so that walkers or wheelchairs don't interfere with access to instruments. Prepare the notational system that will be used so that it can be easily seen and manipulated. Unless you are notating the score in whole by yourself (e.g., for a musician who is playing while you take the musical dictation), make sure that everyone involved can see the score at all times. A large board with large notation is often the better option for keeping everyone in the same place and working together.

Older adults who are composing may find that feelings, emotions, and memories come to the surface during the process. They may need more time for introspection or discussion as a part of the compositional process, especially if issues related to life review are involved. For older adults who are engaging in instrumental composition from an experience orientation, be prepared to work on the composition over an extended time, leaving lots of flexibility for changing the composition as its focus evolves and building in time to take breaks from the process, as it can be cognitively and/or emotionally taxing. If approaching instrumental composition from an outcome orientation, consider structuring the experience so that the focus is clear and defined and the time frame for completion is limited.

Older adults who are musicians may have feelings and emotions arise from changes in their ability to play instruments on which they were once skilled. If a client wishes to compose for their instrument but cannot play it any longer, and if it is not an instrument that you can play, consider what options you might have for this process. Might an electronic program that will play the composition in the sound of the chosen instrument be pleasing to the client, or will this heighten the sense of loss? Should you recommend another instrument? Discuss these issues with the client as they arise so that you can both assist the client in working through the feelings related to the loss and plan and implement a compositional process that will have value and meaning for the client.

Conclusion

Instrumental composition offers affordances for a client or group who will benefit from a therapeutic process that is not couched within language. It provides the chance to sonically explore feelings and issues that may be beyond words or must be explored before words can be accessed. Your careful planning will determine the extent to which any client or group can effectively access the affordances of instrumental composition and will support the effectiveness of the compositional process in producing an instrumental piece that has meaning for the client. Because instrumental composition results in a music score, it can continue to be the target for therapeutic exploration through re-creation. It can also serve as a record of the client's therapeutic process and can be shared with others by the client or group.

9

INSTRUMENTAL COMPOSITION— ILLUSTRATIONS AND EXAMPLES IN THE LITERATURE

Instrumental composition method-variations can be implemented in a variety of ways. This chapter explores the different approaches to planning, designing, implementing, and facilitating instrumental composition methods. The first case illustration in this chapter provides a window into the various clinical decisions that the MT makes and what informs these decisions. Additional case illustrations from the literature demonstrate how the method-variation can be adapted and the structure altered to meet the needs of the client or group. Additionally, a brief review of the literature and research on instrumental composition methods is included. It is worth noting that the literature surrounding instrumental composition in music therapy is sparse, and while it may not be well represented in the literature, this does not mean that it is not used in clinical practice. It is important to understand this method-variation and how it can be utilized to meet a client's therapeutic needs so you can determine if and when it is appropriate in your work with clients.

Composing with a Notational System for Tone Chime Choir with Older Adults in Long-Term Care

Lakeview is a residential retirement community for older adults, offering assisted living and a memory care unit. The MT employed at Lakeview offers a wide variety of music therapy services to the residents. One of the groups available to residents is the tone chime choir. A tone chime is a cylindrical handbell that is smaller, lighter, and easier for older adults to play than traditional handbells. The tone chime choir meets for 60 minutes twice a week. The group uses a 25-note chromatic tone chime set to play the songs they select with the assistance of the MT. The MT selects songs from music genres the group has identified that they like, that have rhythm patterns compatible with the group's current skill level, and that have a musical range that fits within their tone chimes set.

The tone chime choir is an open group, so any Lakeview resident can attend and participate. There are typically 20 to 22 residents who attend the tone chime group each week. Some of the residents have music experience and read music, while others do not; some have some early memory loss and do not always remember the names of notes. The MT has created a color-coded notational system to accommodate the group and ensure that everyone who wants to participate is able to.

The MT designed a notational system that includes a colored sticker (circle-shaped) on each tone chime that is coordinated to a pitch in the melody of the song. The MT color codes the melody of each song for the group. These color-coded melodies are created on a computer so they can then be projected onto a large screen for each member of the group to see during the session. The notation system also uses different sizes of colored circles to indicate the duration of the pitch. For example, a larger circle is four beats; a smaller one represents three beats; still smaller, two beats; and so on.

When the residents arrive for the tone chime choir sessions, they begin doing some gentle arm and hand stretches to music. The MT leads them in this process to help them to warm up to reduce the risk of strain. After the warm-up, the MT introduces the first song the group will practice and projects the color-coded melody on the screen at the front of the room. The MT sings through the melody, pointing to each colored circle on the screen to allow the group to see and hear the tempo and rhythms, as well as to identify the song. The MT then distributes the tone chimes with the color-coded circle stickers so that each resident has a tone chime to play. The MT demonstrates how to play the tone chime so any new participants have the opportunity to learn how to hold and play it. The MT then conducts the group in playing their tone chimes and then stopping the sound as well.

The MT asks the group to look at the colored sticker on their tone chime and find this colored circle up on the screen. The MT then points to each colored circle on the screen one by one and asks each participant to play when she points to their color. This allows the MT to observe whether everyone is connecting the color on their tone chime to the color on the screen when they need to play. They determine their readiness to play the song together as a group.

When the MT is confident that everyone has identified their color on the screen, she moves to the screen and conducts four beats to demonstrate the tempo at which they will play the melody. The MT points to each colored circle in the melody, conducting the group in when to play the next pitch. The group plays through the melody three or four times. This allows the group to learn a new melody and develop a sense of competence in playing.

The MT will use the same notational system and colors for each new song melody. This allows each member of the group to gain a familiarity with the notational system and be able to transfer this knowledge from one melody to another. As the group develops their understanding and skill in using this notational system, they can use it to create their instrumental composition. To do this, the MT has created measures on a white board in the group room. She brings in four different sizes of the various colors of the circles. The melody the group will create will be in 4/4 meter, as this coordinates with the notational system. The MT asks the group to identify the size and color of the circle(s) for measure one. Once the group has placed the circles in the first measure, they play the measure. The MT asks them if they want to change anything about it, such as pitches or the duration of pitches. If not, they move on to the second measure. They repeat the process until they have created the first line of the melody. They play the first line, and the MT checks with the group again to see if they want to make any changes. The group continues this process until they have composed the entire melody. The group plays the entire melody together and, when they are satisfied with their creation, they work together to name their composition.

The notational system the MT created for the tone chime choir was an important adaptation that made this group accessible to residents who did not read music or who may not have been able to recall the names of notes due to memory issues. It allowed the group to play music together to learn the system and develop a sense of competency with it so that they could then use this same system to create their own instrumental composition. The MT scaffolded the process by engaging the group in playing songs that they liked with this notational system, which helped them to develop familiarity with and skills in using this system. This provided them with the confidence to then use this knowledge and skill to create their own composition.

Literature Illustrating Instrumental Composition

MTs adapt composition method-variations in many ways to address various client needs, make composition accessible, and support a client's engagement in the experience. The case provided here highlights what informed the decisions the MT made and how these decisions provided the structure and support the clients needed to engage in the compositional experience.

Cominardi (2014) describes his work with 65 kindergarten children, 14 of whom immigrated from various countries and were demonstrating difficulties integrating into the classroom due to cultural and language barriers that were leading to challenges with behaviors and developing relationships with peers and teachers. To address these issues, all of the children were divided into four groups that participated in music therapy sessions over the course of 7 months. The goals for this therapeutic work included developing relationships with peers, fostering autonomy in self-expression and self-esteem, reducing prejudice and increasing appreciation of diversity, and benefiting from integrated expressive language experiences as a group.

The sessions integrated the use of sound, movement, and color in the space by using Orff and various rhythm instruments, large sheets of paper and pastels, and play furnishings such as slides and benches. The MT utilized these materials to engage the children in three different types of improvisation experiences: sound-musical, graphic-pictorial, and motor-environmental. The improvisation experiences served as the means to create a notation system for the instrumental composition, which integrated sound, movement, and drawings.

In the composition process, the MT encouraged the children to explore the instruments free of directives and constraints. This allowed them to discover new and different ways of communicating through music and sound on the instruments and fostered interactions that reflected the development of new interpersonal relationships. Movement was used to elaborate the various sounds. They then transferred these ideas onto sheets of paper that the group organized in the order that represented the sounds that they wanted in their composition. The final score integrated colors, shapes, and symbols that represented the instrumentation, vocalization, and movement of the composition.

Their composition score was posted on the wall, which became the musical staff for the drawings of their notations. The MT walked the length of the score using a moving bar line, a long stick held in a vertical position, which provided the structure usually provided by meter and bar lines in a traditional music score. In this way, the children were able to experience performing and hearing their composition as a united group. The process of creating their notational system and composition allowed the children to explore new ways of communicating and connecting to one another. It helped them to foster improved relationships with one another and develop a sense of inclusion in the classroom. The opportunity for the children to explore communication and expression in nonverbal ways increased their self-expression and fostered their creativity, which allowed them to co-create their instrumental composition.

Other Literature Related to Instrumental Composition

The literature detailing the use of instrumental composition method-variations is sparse. While there is not a strong body of literature or clinical case studies that provide detailed descriptions of this method-variation in clinical practice, there are different sources that address an aspect of the instrumental composition process. These case examples and literature are included in Table

9.0. The table includes a brief description of the case, details about the focus of the case, and the reference. This is included so you can seek out these sources and review them more fully.

Table 9.0
Case Examples of the Use of Instrumental Composition Method-variations in the Literature

Description of Case	Focus of Case	Reference
Creating piano compositions with pediatric medical care	Clinical vignette of a child undergoing radiation treatment, engaged in composing pieces to play on the piano and playing her compositions for her care team.	O'Callaghan, 2007
Use of instrumental composition methods with children who have experienced trauma	Exploration of ways to structure the instrumental composition process to foster a sense of safety and security when working with traumatized children.	LaVerdiere, 2007
Creating instrumental compositions with hospitalized children and adolescents	Description of the process of supporting pediatric patients in creating instrumental compositions to support relaxation, provide procedural support, and manage pain and anxiety.	Bradt, 2014
Engaging caregivers in instrumental composition process	Procedures and adaptations to support caregivers in the compositional process.	Daveson, 2014
Group instrumental composition process in creating music to support meditation	A detailed description of the group composition process utilized to create instrumental music to support meditation practices. Many musical and instrumental considerations are included.	Heiderscheit, 2014
Instrumental composition with children with	Considerations, procedures, and adaptations when	Soikia, 2014a, 2014b

developmental delays	designing composition experiences for children with developmental delays. Brief case illustrations included.	
Creating the music to support the client's lyric content in hip-hop songs	Description of the MT's process in assisting the 11-year-old client with a spinal cord injury in creating the music to support his lyric content and expressions	Viega, 2015
Techniques for creating the music for compositions	Ideas and suggestions for ways to approach the process of creating the melody and harmonic aspects of a composition, including brief case illustrations and tools to be utilized to support clients in the process	Aasgaard & Blichfeldt Ærø, 2016
Process of co-creating music with Israeli, Palestinian, and Palestinian-Israeli youth as a means of transformation from conflict	Detailing a process of music creation and -making with youth through a nonprofit organization to address issues of social injustice and explore social equity and conflict transformation	Gottesman, 2017

Summary

Instrumental composition method-variations provide the opportunity for a client or group of clients to create music without the need for language. The MT can creatively adapt and structure this process to meet the unique needs, skills, abilities, interests, and preferences of a client. The case illustrations in this chapter demonstrate the creative ways in which this method-variation can be adapted for different clients—even those who do not read music. This literature also represents the different clinical settings in which MTs are implementing instrumental composition method-variations.

References

Aasgaard, T., & Blichfeldt Ærø, S. (2016). Songwriting techniques in music therapy practice. In J. Edwards (Ed.), *The Oxford handbook of music therapy* (pp. 644–668). Oxford University Press.

Bradt, J. (2014). Pain management and children. In J. Bradt (Ed.), *Guidelines for music therapy practice in pediatric care* (pp. 15–65). Barcelona Publishers.

Cominardi, C. (2014). From creative process to transcultural process: Integrating music therapy with arts media in Italian kindergartens—A pilot study. *Australian Journal of Music Therapy, 25,* 3–14.

Daveson, B. (2014). Caring for caregivers. In J. Allen (Ed.), *Guidelines for music therapy practice in adult medical care* (pp. 347–363). Barcelona Publishers.

Gottesman, S. (2016). Hear and be heard: learning with and through music as a dialogical space for co-creating youth-led conflict transformation. *Voices: A world forum for music therapy, 17*(1). https://doi.org/10.15845/voices.v17i1.857

Heiderscheit, A. (2014). Spiritual practices. In L. Eyre (Ed.) *Guidelines for music therapy practice in mental health* (pp. 873–901). Barcelona Publishers.

LaVerdiere, E. (2007). The use of music therapy with children who have been sexually abused. In S. Brooke (Ed.), *The use of the creative therapies with sexual abuse survivors* (pp. 207–234). Charles C. Thomas Publishers.

O'Callaghan, C., Sexton, M., & Wheeler, G. (2007). Music therapy as a nonpharmacological anxiolytic for paediatric radiotherapy patients. *Australasian Radiology, 51*(2), 159–162.

Sokira, J. (2014a). Rett Syndrome. In M. Hinz (Ed.), *Guidelines for music therapy practice in developmental health* (pp. 87–107). Barcelona Publishers.

Sokira, J. (2014b). Physical disabilities in school children. In M. Hinz (Ed.), *Guidelines for music therapy practice in developmental health* (pp. 370–389). Barcelona Publishers.

Viega, M. (2015). Working with the negatives to make a better picture: Creating hip-hop songs in pediatric rehabilitation. In C. Dileo (Ed.), *Advanced practice in medical music therapy: Case reports* (pp. 46–60). Jeffrey Books/Music Therapy Resources.

10

MUSIC COLLAGE

Music collage is a method-variation that involves the selection of sounds, songs, and music and their intentional sequencing to create a recording with a specific therapeutic focus. Music collage may offer more possibilities than any of the other compositional method-variations because so many different musical and other art modalities can be incorporated into the compositional process. In fact, you may find that you and the client or group make use of other method-variations as a part of composing a collage. In the process of selecting and sequencing musical material focused on a particular therapeutic topic, you can assist the client in exploring and working through related thoughts, feelings, relationships, and behavioral patterns. The final recorded product becomes a concrete expression of this exploration and can serve as a record of the work done during the therapeutic process. Other arts modalities can be added to the creation process resulting in multimedia products. Because you have a wide range of structure that can be applied to this method-variation, it can be a good choice for engaging many clients of varying ability levels. Like other compositional products, a music collage may be re-experienced multiple times, may be kept by the client as a reminder or memento, and can be easily shared with others if the client so chooses. A music collage might serve many purposes, including, but not limited to ...

- An exploration of a single therapeutic topic
- A record of self-reflection related to the identification and expression of feelings and emotions

- The exploration and resolution of a particular life event or relationship
- A creation related to the acquisition of academic or other cognitive skills addressed within music therapy
- The outcome of the practice of social skills within a group
- Life review or review of a particular time of life
- An exploration of identity
- The creation of a record commemorating a relationship in or out of the therapeutic setting
- A commemorative or legacy gift expressing the thoughts and feelings of the creator about the recipient

Prerequisites

Clients must have the ability to make choices and to communicate them to participate in a music collage experience. They must have some receptive language capacity in order to understand and respond to the therapeutic focus of the compositional process. Beyond this, however, it will be the choices that you make in structuring the collage experience that make it accessible and appropriate for the client's therapeutic involvement. Properly assessing the client's capability in terms of communication, cognitive processing, and musical knowledge and skill will help you to prepare materials that circumvent difficulties in participation outside of these few prerequisites.

Risks and Contraindications

Creating a music collage requires a significant amount of decision-making on the part of the client or group. Clients might become frustrated or angry if they begin to feel overwhelmed by this demand, especially if they have too many choices or if the topic is not focused enough for them to identify their own thoughts and feelings in relation to it. You can mitigate this risk by carefully considering how you prepare the client or group prior to introducing the collage experience and by your consideration of what structures you provide within the collage process to offer enough decision-making to challenge them without exceeding their capabilities.

Group music collages require group decision-making and conflict resolution and at times may require comfort with self-disclosure within the group. With a group that has new members or in which little cohesion has been formed, the collage process may need to be limited to superficial topics that allow comfort and cohesion to grow. Trying to address deeper issues when there is not sufficient safety within the group will not result in effective exploration. In addition, when group members lack the necessary degree of social skills to engage with others with respect and a willingness to work out differences of opinion, a group music collage may not be a good choice of method-variation.

In the music collage experience, the client or group is being asked to focus on a particular topic related to their therapeutic process. Exploring therapeutic topics through the medium of music always has the potential risk of bringing up uncomfortable or disturbing memories and feelings. It can trigger individuals who associate specific sounds or music with a painful memory, a damaging behavior or craving, or a past trauma. You can decrease the chance of these risks, again, with careful preparation of the client for the collage process and consideration of how you structure and give directives for the experience. If clients have the capability for more freedom in exploring the sound and music resources for composing a collage—such as the use of loops and other electronically created sound, recordings of their own improvisations or original compositions, and so forth—you must remain alert for indications that sounds or music may have unexpectedly led to a difficult, upsetting, or trauma-related response in the client. No matter how long you might have worked with a client, it is not possible to understand everything that might be triggering for them. You must be prepared to work through and resolve these types of responses from the client or to have immediate access to someone who can assist with this process. Otherwise, limit the amount of creative sound and music resources for the collage to those with which you and the client have already worked in previous sessions.

Affordances and Challenges

Decision-making. As with all of the compositional method-variations, music collage offers the client the affordance of decision-making. The importance of decision-making for the client might be functional (e.g., practicing the skill of making choices), communicative (e.g., making one's expressions clear to others), role rehearsing (e.g., expressively asserting oneself), or collaborative (e.g., learning to negotiate choices within a group), or it might be the end result of an insight or resolution of a conflict. Even if you have selected a music collage experience for your client or group for some other reason, the collage process will help the client to develop and strengthen decision-making skills.

Self-awareness. The creative process involved in selecting and combining sounds and music to make a meaningful music collage requires awareness of one's own thoughts, feelings, preferences, and wishes. This awareness may range from the simple (e.g., Do I like this? or Is this how I want this to sound?) to the complex and soul-searching (e.g., How does this reflect my identity? or Will this help someone else to understand my feelings?). This affordance of the music collage process makes it an excellent choice for clients whose therapeutic process is focused on developing better awareness of self or for whom self-awareness must be increased in order to effectively address a larger treatment problem. The composed product that results from the collage process serves as a concrete representation and reminder of what the client has discovered about themselves.

Self-expression. Music collage may be the most accessible of all of the compositional method-variations because any sound source and any source of improvised, composed, performed, and/or recorded music are all potentially available to the client as compositional material. The client need not have any music training or education in order to compose a collage, which allows them to have as much creative freedom in the creation process as their strengths and limitations allow. On the other hand, for the client to create freely and express themselves without any specific music knowledge, you must know how to utilize the resources that allow this, such as digital sound and music sources, computers, recording equipment, and other technology. You may need to seek out some continuing education—or even just help from a colleague who is technologically savvy—to stay on top of the newest developments in technology so that you are prepared to offer your clients the support they might need in a freely creative collage process. Again, Chapter 12 provides more information regarding this.

Self-reflection and reminiscence. The process of music collage can afford the client the opportunity to reflect on their own experiences, whether these are focused on specific events, behavioral or interactional patterns, relationships, a particular time of life, or a full life review. Re-creating feelings, experiences, and memories in sound and music allows the client to put into a more concrete form the meaning that they associate with these aspects of their life and to consider, question, re-evaluate, relive, rethink, and resolve them for integration into their own identity. For example, in working through a grief process, a client may combine parts of meaningful songs, evocative recorded sounds, and recorded verbal reminiscences related to the loss in order to commit important aspects to memory, celebrate the value of the relationship that was lost, and understand what it means to continue on without that relationship.

Communication. The concrete nature of the collage composition also allows the client to share meanings and understandings of their life experiences with others as a part of their therapeutic process or to develop support, reaffirm, or resolve conflict within these relationships. For example, in end-of-life care, the MT may help the client to assemble a collage of music that they wish to give to family members or loved ones as a legacy gift that communicates to them their love and affection in a format that will endure after their passing. Similarly, members of a therapy group that is coming to a close may compose a collage together that represents each member of the group and places them sonically in relation to each other as a means of communicating the value of the group in each of their processes. Because the collage composition process can incorporate other arts media in combination with sound media, the multimedia collage can serve as a communication of thoughts and feelings that are highly complex and cannot be fully expressed through a single medium.

Cooperation and conflict resolution. While working as a group to compose a music collage, objectives related to group decision-making, tolerance and respect for different ideas, and effectively resolving disagreements can be addressed. The group process allows for measurement of change with regard to relational behavior patterns that may be targeted, as can individual objectives related to assertiveness, frustration tolerance, and other social skills. A music collage process that addresses these types of social and group behaviors might result in a collage that is a grouping of individual contributions or a single product in which individual contributions are melded into a single sonic picture. Again, the wide array of available resources (e.g., live and recorded sound, electronics, art media) and the multitude of choices for structuring the composition processes afford social experiences to improve cooperation and conflict resolution for clients at many levels of capability.

Orientations to Clinical Decision-Making

Outcome Orientation

Music collages can be useful and effective within an outcome orientation in a number of ways. Predetermined treatment objectives might be addressed through the process of creating the collage, through the content of the collage, or through the intended use of the collage after its completion. In the latter case, the creation of the music collage might be considered pretherapeutic, or a step that is necessary in order to stimulate or assist in change. The MT may use the resource materials of music collage, the directives that guide the collage composition process, the predetermined focus of the music collage, or the use of the final product as the means to address cognitive, behavioral, or social growth and development.

Music as agent. A music collage composition can act as an agent when it serves to reinforce or manage behaviors or mood states. For example, the client who experiences insomnia because of anxiety may work with the MT to create a collage that combines specific music that they have found to be relaxing and distracting; the client then uses this music product on their own at times when anxiety is interrupting sleep. The process of creating a music collage might serve as a reinforcer of positive social behaviors for the client, who must follow group rules and interact appropriately with others in order to contribute to the composition. In this case, the motivating nature of music composition is the positive reinforcer for the client who is practicing new social behaviors.

Music as skill. The music collage process places demands on those involved that the MT can direct and shape to assist the client in the development of emotional and social skills. Issues such as frustration tolerance, emotion regulation, communication, and conflict resolution are prime candidates for skill development through collage composition. The teenage client who struggles with frustration and anger management difficulties, for example, may be afforded the chance to work on mediating these emotional states as they learn to use a computer and other electronics to create a collage that expresses their feelings. Not only is the emotion management addressed by the collage process, but also the client might even develop skills that inspire future career aspirations (e.g., computer science or music industry studies).

Music therapy protocols. The music collage process also lends itself to objectives-based, time-limited treatment. For example, a client with a chronic mental illness may need to define a plan for illness management prior to their discharge date from the hospital. The MT might involve the client in a compositional process in which the following steps are completed: (1) identify problematic behaviors and habits, (2) identify feelings and emotions related to these behaviors and habits, (3) identify healthy responses to these behaviors and feelings, (4) identify support systems to assist in these healthy responses, and (5) identify a motivating wish for the future to encourage perseverance in illness management. The MT and client may compose an album made of short collages for each of these steps in the management plan or perhaps might compose one collage that represents the progression through each step. The final collage then not only identifies when and how the client met the objectives for completing the illness management plan but also provides a concrete reminder of the plan for the client when they are discharged and can make use of it.

Experience Orientation

From an experience-oriented perspective, the music collage process allows the client exploratory space and resources from which they can identify thoughts, feelings, problems, and issues that relate to their overall therapeutic process. Since creativity is, in and of itself, a problem-solving process (i.e., a process in which decisions must be made, whether consciously or unconsciously), the freedom of exploration and expression in the composition of a music collage affords the client potential access to their own inner experiences in ways that they may not be able to access in typical daily life, presenting the client with new information and new perspectives on themselves that can be used as material for therapeutic work.

Music as process. The fluid nature of therapeutic processes and the flexibility to make clinical decisions from a methods-based perspective are particularly highlighted in the use of music collage. It may not be highly common for a MT and client to start with a compositional collage as a means of helping the client to identify their focus for treatment, but any active engagement in music may naturally transition into a collage process. For example, while singing preferred songs together, the client may begin to express concerns that suggest to the MT that they can create the opportunity for clarifying those concerns and stimulating deeper exploration of them through a collage process. Or, the exploration that occurs in the collage process may naturally transition into another method-variation, such as when the client improvises on the piano to help in making creative decisions for the music collage. The improvisation might be recorded and used as a new sound source for the collage, or it might lead into a separate exploration of therapeutic material in future sessions.

Regardless of where the music collage enters into or transitions within the client's therapeutic process, its highly creative nature provides a bridge to internal experiences and possibly to unconscious material that is ready to move into consciousness. Furthermore, it gives these thoughts, feelings, and experiences a concrete form that may facilitate better exploration and understanding by the client. It is the MT's responsibility, then, to provide the structures that assist the client in their exploration and to contain the experience so that safety is maintained and the focus remains on the issues that are most relevant to the client's treatment needs.

Music as representation. The music collage itself, as a product, is highly representational in nature and can range from the simple (This represents what I like) to the highly complex (This represents how I find meaning and value in my life experiences). In the example mentioned above regarding the affordance of communication, the individual coming to terms with a terminal illness might use a music collage composition as a means to represent their thoughts and feelings relative to the people who are most important in their life. In creating a collage that communicates this about each important individual, the client builds a record of the value of these relationships in their life and explores how they have given their life meaning. The resulting product, when presented to the loved ones to whom it is directed, then stands as a concrete representation of the client even after they have passed. This is particularly true when the collage contains recordings of the client's own music performance or verbalizations. The music collage is a sonic picture that potentially leaves a lasting marker of the meaning ascribed to its contents.

Procedural Guidelines and Considerations

You will need to consider a number of things once you decide that a music collage is an appropriate choice of experience to offer your client or group. Remember that you must temper your ideas for how to engage the client or group in this process with an awareness of your capabilities and limitations in using certain resources. With other method-variations that largely utilize the music skills that you develop as a student of music therapy, making a compositional process for collage accessible for some clients might require that you utilize skills that exceed the boundaries of typical music therapy education. In particular, you may need to have more than just a cursory knowledge of music electronics and other technology in order to effectively involve some clients in the compositional process. It is recommended that you make a plan for yourself to continue increasing your awareness of and ability to use technology in music therapy sessions so that you are not limited in your use of this method-variation. Chapter 12 may help you to identify technology and skill areas that you can work to develop.

Again, the guidelines and procedures that follow are generally involved in the music collage process. There may be other steps you take to plan or structure the experience, adapt it, evaluate it, and so forth. The better you know your client and the more aware you are of the materials and resources you have in your repertoire, the more options you may find in your own planning and implementation of music collage.

Planning

- Determine your client's specific abilities and limitations in relation to participating in a music collage experience, including all the relevant domains of functioning.
    - Concrete or abstract thinking?
    - Reading and writing capability?
    - Able to attend, and for how long?
    - Able to work with others?
    - Musical preferences?
    - Musical experience?
    - Musical knowledge?
    - Technology knowledge and skill?

- Consider how much time you have to assist the client in completing the collage process and limit the resources that you are prepared to offer to those that will facilitate completion within that time.

- Determine what personal and material resources you have available to assist the client in the music collage process.
    - What equipment do you have available to work with recorded material, and do you know how to set it up and use it? Enlist help during your planning process if you need to learn how to connect or use your equipment— and practice beforehand!
    - Do you have an instrumentarium that provides a wide choice for instrumental music creation?

- Do you have a computer that is accessible to clients that does not contain access to protected or forbidden content, such as personal client information or session documentation or Internet access that is disallowed for your particular setting?
- Do you have apps and programs at your disposal that clients can use for electronic composition?
- Do you have access to a broad selection of prerecorded music, sounds, and loops?
- Do you want to be able to offer other arts media to incorporate into the collage process, and do you have these materials and the appropriate space in which to use them?
- Are all of the materials and resources you want to offer to your clients appropriate and safe for them to use? Are there some that you will offer to use *for* them because of safety issues?

• Consider whether your client will need some sort of adaptive equipment or other adaptive resources in order to compose the collage.
  - Physical adaptive equipment for playing, such as special mallets or instrument-stabilizing devices?
  - Adaptive communication equipment to assist with verbal communication?
  - A means for using adaptive notation to plan live music for recording?

• Set up your therapy space so that all options that you want to offer to your client can be accessed with minimal disruption to the session.

• Be prepared with examples or suggestions to help your client or group to think about what they want their final collage to be.

• Be prepared with materials to make a "map" of the collage as it is being composed.
  - Paper and pens or pencils?
  - White board and markers?
  - Poster board and Post-It notes?

176 Compositional Methods in Music Therapy

- Journals for a long-term collage project?

In the table that follows there is a listing of possible client and therapist roles that may assist you in thinking about the various possibilities for which you may need to prepare when planning a music collage experience.

Table 10.0
Considerations for Planning a Music Collage Experience

Client's Capabilities	Client's Role	Therapist's Role
Moderate to severe cognitive limitation	chooses content	provides a selection from which the client chooses
	if appropriate, decides about recorded live performance	performs and records selected live music
	chooses to sing and/or play and picks instrumentation for recorded live performance	provides appropriate supportive accompaniment for client performance; makes suggestions for inclusion of client's singing or playing
	chooses order of music selections or sounds	facilitates client's decision-making by giving examples or playing different options
	decides about inclusion of other arts modalities	makes suggestions for incorporation of other arts and facilitates the client's completion; incorporates it into the final recording in an appropriate format
Mild to moderate cognitive limitation	chooses content	provides options for what might be included, including prerecorded music, sounds, and/or live recordings
	chooses what, if any, of the content should be recorded from live performance	provides options for what is reasonable for recorded live performance
	decides to what extent they will sing and/or play	performs and records selections or provides

	for recorded live performances, and on instrumentation	appropriate accompaniment for client's singing and playing
	decides about inclusion of other arts modalities	offers available media choices and assists client's decision-making regarding how the content fits into the final product; formats it for inclusion to meet client's specifications
	participates in exploring the arrangement of music and sounds for the final product	provides technical support for the client to work with the arrangement of recorded material
No cognitive limitations	chooses content	provides access to all sources for music and sounds; offers options for recording live music and sounds; provides assistance with computer, apps, and other electronic equipment
	decides on live performance of content for recording and enlists MT to assist with performance of selections if necessary	assists in use of available recording equipment for the recording process; provides live musical support as requested by the client
	decides about inclusion of other arts modalities	provides available media; assists client in using chosen media to support musical exploration of the topic at hand*
	creates the final plan for the collage product	assists by keeping client's wishes within the limits of available resources for creating the final product; provides reasonable options for final production
	uses recording and computer technology to	assists the client with resources and technology as

	the extent possible to make the final product	necessary
Musical skill	chooses all content	provides resources and clarifies the limitations of these resources and equipment
	performs live content for recording and enlists MT to assist with performance to client's specifications	makes necessary instruments available; assists in use of available recording equipment for the recording process; provides live musical support as requested by the client
	decides about inclusion of other arts modalities	provides available media; assists client in using chosen media to support musical exploration of the topic at hand*
	creates the final plan for the collage product	assists by keeping client's wishes within the limits of available resources for creating the final product; provides reasonable options for final production
	uses recording and computer technology to the extent possible to make the final product	assists the client with resources and technology as necessary
Technology skill	chooses all content	provides resources and clarifies the limitations of these resources and equipment
	decides on live performance of content for recording and enlists MT to assist with performance of selections if necessary	assists in use of available recording equipment for the recording process; provides live musical support as requested by the client
	decides on live performance of content for recording and enlists MT to assist with	assists in use of available recording equipment for the recording process; provides live musical support as

performance of selections if necessary	requested by the client
produces the final collage product	assists the client with resources and access to technology as necessary

Remember to stay within the limits of your training and education. MTs are not qualified to use other expressive arts as the primary medium for therapeutic processes unless properly credentialed in that modality.

Engaging

- Describe the purpose of composing a music collage and assist your client or group in clarifying the specific focus for or intent of the composition.

- Describe the different aspects involved in making a music collage. Decide together with your client or group how complex the collage will be and what roles each of you will take. Realize that this may change as you go along if you are working from an experience-oriented perspective and let your clients know that they can change their minds about this within the time and resource restraints available to them.

- Introduce the client to the different materials with which they can work in the collage process. Demonstrate what they might do with different computer programs or digital apps and video equipment. Let them know the extent to which they can create or re-create music themselves and how you might use these recordings.

- If clients are capable of using the computer, electronic apps, and video equipment, spend time giving them a tutorial on what can be done with them and how they operate. If possible, let them have time to practice using these resources so they feel comfortable with them.

- Be clear about exactly which resources they can use in the process and which they cannot; for example, if you are using prerecorded music but do not have the equipment to convert analog recordings to digital, let your client know that they can select music from any CD or the available streaming service but not from the analog LPs that are in the room.

- Begin the composition process by brainstorming ideas around the therapeutic topic at hand, including songs, music, and sounds that the client might identify with the content.

- Keep a record of the ideas for the collage as they develop and start a working map of how the collage might be put together. If possible, have the group, a group-chosen individual, or the client make a record of the ideas and keep the map updated.

- If you have recordings of the client or group singing, playing, or improvising from previous sessions, make these available for use if appropriate to the topic under exploration.

- If the clients want to use video or other arts media, assist them with using the media or the equipment and help them to remain focused on the topic at hand with these creations. It is important to remember to remain within the limits of our training and education where the inclusion of other arts media is concerned. While the inclusion of drawings or writings may be in support of the music collage process, MTs are not trained to use these other art media as a primary means of therapeutic process. The focus must remain on the exploration through musical means, with other media highlighting what is discovered within this music process.

- Help clients who have good verbal and writing skills and may have kept a journal in relation to the collage process to distill their thoughts and expressions that are most important to the final product. Assist them in deciding how these will be included in the final product.
    - Album liner notes?
    - Verbiage added to art?
    - Signs or captions added to video?
    - Spoken recordings incorporated into the music?

- When all decisions have been made, assist the clients in preparing the final recording. With clients without the capacity or skill to put together the final product, you may need to complete this step on your own to bring back to the clients in the next session.

Observing

- Keep the client focused on the exploration of the issue at hand. The use of creative processes can be fun and may lead the client or group to unintentionally avoid the therapeutic issue in the midst of working with creative material.
    - Are the musical choices being made directly in relation to the exploration of the therapeutic topic?
    - Is the discussion remaining focused on the topic, or is it veering off into discussion of likes and dislikes of unrelated material?
    - Should you refocus discussion?
    - Is the discussion moving in a different direction that indicates a deeper issue that should alter the exploration for the collage?

- Notice how the client problem-solves during the experience and make note of where they demonstrate difficulty or frustration.
    - Is the difficulty or frustration with the completion of the steps of the collage process, the topic of the collage, or the feelings that the process elicits?
    - Is there indication that a trauma response has been triggered?

- Make note of the client's or group's reactions to the plan and the final product as it develops.
    - Is there pride or contentment with the content?
    - Are feelings, emotions, and memories elicited that should be further explored?
    - Does it appear that parts of the collage need to be adjusted in some way?

Adapting

- Consider the extent and quality of your client's participation or of each client's participation in the group. Are they having difficulty in fully engaging in the creative process? If so, why is this? How can you change the structure of the experience to increase their active engagement?
    - Have they lost interest because it is too easy or too hard?
    - Do they understand what they are being asked to do and why?

- Consider how the experience is unfolding. Is the experience effectively addressing the concern it was meant to address? Might there be new or deeper therapeutic information that is being revealed by the creative process?
    - Might you give choices or ask questions to bring client awareness to the most pertinent issue?
    - Might you offer a different perspective to what is being created?
    - Should you help to refocus the collage on the newly revealed issue? If so, how might you help in the restructuring of what has already been planned?
    - Is there an indication that another method-variation might be called for in service of the new issue?
    - Might another method-variation be incorporated into the current collage process in order to address new material?

Developing

- Consider how you might help to deepen the exploration by elaboration on the aspect or topic at hand.
    - Has the client or group finished the process without adding any depth to their awareness of understanding in relation to the issue at hand?
    - Might the incorporation of other arts media provide opportunity to more deeply access the affordance of the music process?
    - Should you suggest layering of music and other media to encourage deeper exploration?

- Consider whether there is indication that the collage process might move beyond its initial intended limits and bring about a larger exploration.
    - Is an expansion of the collage timeline or content warranted by newly discovered insights?
    - Might the process continue on to the next step of therapeutic process—for example, from identifying feelings and emotions to exploring behavioral patterns around them?

Accompanying

- Consider whether the client or group might be avoiding expressions they would like to make because of concern about lack of musical or technical skill. Make sure to point out different musical additions you are willing to offer if desired for the collage, such as live performance, musical accompaniment, or your use of some technology to help the client to create an expression they want.

- As with all compositional method-variations, remember that the final product must reflect the client or group, not you. Offer all of the help that the clients need but be judicious in determining how your additions or musical and technical support highlight their therapeutic process.

Reviewing

- You might consider reviewing the final plan prior to making the collage product.
    - In looking at the whole, does the client or group feel as though it is complete?
    - Should alterations be made to make it more accurate?
    - In a group project, does each client feel as though they are adequately represented within the collage?
    - Are there aesthetic changes that should be made to allow for the client's fullest and most accurate expression?
    - If the client or group is unhappy with the expected outcome, are there aspects that can be changed to satisfy them?

- Encourage the client or group to share and explore their reactions to the final music collage product.
  - How does it feel to experience the final whole?
  - What did they learn in the process, and what meaning does this have now that the process is complete?
  - Does the completed product bring up new thoughts and feelings? Does it lead to another step in the client's or group's therapeutic process?

- Discuss the initial intended use for the final project.
  - If the intention was for sharing, is it still appropriate to share the collage? In a group, is everyone comfortable with sharing it outside of the session? Are the initial intended recipients for the collage still appropriate? Are there others who should be included in the sharing who weren't previously considered?
  - Ensure that the group agrees on and promises to follow the agreement about the final disposition of their music collage. Review any existing group rules about confidentiality.

Closing

- Provide the client or each client in the group a copy of their final music collage.

- In a group, review the agreements made about where, how, and with whom the contents should be shared.

- It is a good ending to experience the music collage as a whole one more time in closing the process, unless it has been decided by the client or group that the process has led to a resolution that does not need to be re-experienced.

Special Considerations

With children. Always consider the developmental level of children with regard to cognition, language development, abstract thought, and so on. Consider how the music collage process is helpful to their therapeutic needs within these natural limitations. You might want to plan on preparing visual aids that can be used in the planning process or to help them to remember the topic to which their music choices are related. You will need to limit choices to keep the process focused and useful relative to the issue at hand. Also, consider which resources are appropriate and accessible for children. For example, if you are using Internet-based resources, how will you manage this usage so that clients do not access inappropriate content? While children are learning to use electronic resources at very young ages, their familiarity with electronics does not always translate in their ability to use them in focused, functional ways. Let them know what can be done to create their collage and outline which parts you will be able to do for them when they have made their choices.

With adolescents. You may find that adolescents will take particular interest in a music collage process and that they can exercise a great deal of free expression through this method-variation. This is very useful because adolescents do not always have the words to explain the complex nature of their thoughts and feelings. This, of course, also creates the possibility for inappropriate or even harmful expression. Make sure that you have developed rules with the client or group that outline what is acceptable within the various forms of expression and what is not. In the case of clients or groups who are seen in residential or treatment program settings, ensure that you have reviewed the rules existing for that milieu. If the rules of the unit, facility, or agency are not followed and/or the client or the group shares their collage work outside of the session, this may result in unexpected consequences for them and may hinder their trust in you. Adolescents are even more well versed in electronic resources than are children. You will need to consider how to make sure that they access only online resources that are at safe and reliable sites.

Adolescents' knowledge and skill with electronic resources and media may also provide an additional potential benefit. In the process of creating music collages, there may be opportunities for adolescent clients to teach you a thing or two about cutting-edge technology or to complete some complex work utilizing electronic resources. This may be a significant source of pride for them and may build feelings of competence that are valuable secondary outcome to the main therapeutic focus of the music collage process.

Discussion about how, where, and with whom music collages are shared may be especially important for adolescents because therapeutic content related to identity will not be uncommon. Additionally, expressions of difficult thoughts and feelings that are carefully processed in a therapy setting may, without proper context, seem threatening or worrisome to others. Assist your clients in thinking through when it is safe to share personal thoughts, feelings, and revelations with others and which people will be ready to accept their expressions with healthy support and encouragement.

With older adults. Older adults are the least likely to be well versed in electronic equipment and applications. If this is part of what you have to offer in the music collage process for an older adult or group, make sure that you present options in a manner that makes it clear which use of technology you will complete for them and for which you will provide immediate assistance. You want to provide as much structure as they need to help them to feel competent in completing the selection and arrangement of the collage.

Music is very closely tied to our identities, and for older adults who are selecting and arranging music and sounds in relation to events and relationships in their own lives, it is possible that memories that are emotionally charged or difficult to experience may arise. Be prepared to take the necessary time to support the client in acknowledging and working through any such feelings that might come up in relation to the creative process. For this reason, approaching the collage process from an experience orientation may be much more useful for an older adult or group than it would be from an outcome orientation. Addressing issues as they emerge from the process creates the opportunity for resolution of internal conflicts that can result in a more meaningful experience that is solidified in the final music collage product.

When focusing on life review in the music collage process with older adults, be mindful of the time that is available and the energy that the individual has within any given session. Structure the project in such a way that the demands are spread over a reasonable amount of time or plan on doing smaller projects of a more focused nature that can be completed expediently. If these music collages are intended to be given to or shared with the clients' family or loved ones, make sure that you have gotten information about the needed format for the final product. With younger people, you may produce a digital recording, but for older adults, you may need to plan on an audio or video recording that is copied onto a CD. Talk with your clients about their needs for sharing early in the collage process so that you can arrange to complete the product in the needed format.

Conclusion

Music collage provides a wide array of choices for client engagement for many different therapeutic purposes. Because music in almost all formats—prerecorded, live recorded, electronic, and so forth—can be used to create the collage and because the freely expressive format of music collage allows for the incorporation of other method-variations and other expressive arts media, the opportunity for client exploration and expression around therapeutic topics is almost unlimited. The MT must know both what resources they have available to offer their clients in the collage process and how to use these resources so that they can structure a collage experience that is fully accessible and results in a product that is satisfying to the client while meeting their therapeutic needs.

11

MUSIC COLLAGE – ILLUSTRATIONS AND EXAMPLES IN THE LITERATURE

Music Collage with a Man with Neurodevelopmental Disability

David was a 26-year-old man with developmental limitations and a diagnosis of autism. He had been admitted to a mental health hospital for treatment of depression, the symptoms of which included extreme irritability and violent outbursts. David's cognitive functioning was at the level of a 4-year-old, and his speech was significantly limited. He typically communicated with others by saying yes, no, and nodding his head. He was unable to read or write and could count only to 5. When David came to music therapy, his expected length of stay in the facility was 10 days. Three individual music therapy sessions were planned within that time.

  The treatment team had sent David to music therapy in order to provide him with ways to express his feelings and emotions. His irritability and violent outbursts also suggested that he would benefit from exercising some control within his daily experience. The treatment objectives for David included making choices and expressing his feelings. During the initial assessment, the MT noted that David responded affectively and attended carefully to recorded music that was familiar to him. Hearing songs he knew and liked quickly brightened his mood and seemed to energize him in a positive way. Given the very short time they had to work together and considering David's interactive limitations, the MT chose to use his preferred recorded music as a means to build a relationship with David and to provide him with opportunities to express himself in whatever ways he was able—musically, nonverbally, and/or verbally. The MT knew that David would require a high level of structure and a process that could be shaped with concrete directives, so she chose to offer David the option of composing his own album of music to take with him when he was discharged and to which he could then listen whenever he needed it. David indicated to her that he would like to do that.

David had immediately walked to the record albums when he first entered the room and had shown great interest in the pictures on the covers; hence the MT began by prompting David to look through the records and CDs that were in the treatment room and to find albums he recognized and liked. When he showed interest in one, she would ask him if he liked a song on the album. David would sometimes indicate that he did not, and the MT would clarify by asking whether he just liked the picture. In this way, as they looked through the large selection of albums available, they identified a number of albums he recognized because he associated them with songs.

To start selecting the music that David wanted to compile, the MT played excerpts from the albums they had identified. David could not talk about which songs he liked or read the song titles, so the MT picked better-known songs from each to sample for David. As they listened, she would watch David's affect closely for changes that suggested the music felt good to him. When she saw affective changes, she questioned David: "Do you like this song?" "Does it feel good when you hear it?" "If you were feeling badly and you heard this song, would it help you to feel better?" "Is this a song that you want on your album?"

David and the MT continued this process for two sessions. By the end of the second session, they had worked together to narrow down the choices to five songs that he had indicated in both sessions that he wanted to keep. The MT then wanted to encourage David to express something about the music he had chosen. Their limited time together did not allow an effective exploration of instruments for improvisation, so the MT chose to incorporate another creative art as an alternative means for David to use to express something about his chosen music. She provided him with white paper and oil pastels, and, while they listened to his song selections, she prompted David to draw something that looked the way his music made him feel inside. What David drew appeared to be water and fish.

> MT: David, are those fish in the water?
> *David nods yes.*
> MT: They look like dolphins to me.
> *David smiles at the therapist and nods.*
> MT: Do swimming dolphins match how your music makes you feel inside?
> *David is silent for a while and then looks at the therapist: "They're free."*
> MT: Listening to your favorite music makes you feel free inside?
> *David smiles and nods.*

Before concluding this final session, the MT laid out the albums from which David's selections were taken and asked him to choose the order in which he wanted his songs to play. David picked by pointing to the albums. After the session, the MT transferred David's selections onto a blank CD by using a computer for selections from prerecorded CDs and a turntable connected to the computer for selections from LP records that required digitizing. She then made a reduced-size color copy of David's drawing to insert into the CD case as his album cover. As David was being discharged from the hospital, the MT met with him to say good-bye and to present him with a recording of what he had composed.

This case illustration—taken with permission from a chapter by Jackson (2018b) in *Introduction to Music Therapy Practice* (Heiderscheit & Jackson, 2018)—demonstrates a highly structured, outcome-oriented music collage experience. The MT chose this method-variation because it can be made concrete and be structured to meet treatment objectives within a limited time frame. Simultaneously, it can also allow the client's personal expressions despite significant limitations. The music collage experience afforded David the agency to make choices that expressed his preferences and ultimately allowed him to express something about his own feelings and emotions that he might not have been able to express in a different format, given his cognitive limitations. It also made it possible to address the pre-identified treatment objectives.

This illustration also shows the far end of a very broad range of choices for a composed product that is offered by music collage. In other circumstances, a compilation of prerecorded songs might not seem to fit the definition of a music composition; however, David's limitations in verbal expression and his concrete thought processes required a level of structure that would permit his active engagement in the process. The selection and arrangement of all precomposed, prerecorded material provided him with this structure. David's interaction with the music also afforded him a level of self-awareness that circumvented his limitations, resulting in a surprisingly—almost shockingly—abstract understanding of his internal experience: a feeling of freedom that he represented by swimming dolphins. It is the MT's understanding of how to provide the appropriate level of structure within the music collage experience that provides the client with the opportunity to freely interact with the music in such a way.

At the time this case illustration occurred, it was relatively new for most music therapy clinicians to be using much technology in or around sessions. The recordable CD and the turntable with a USB plug-in that allowed for analog-to-digital recording were considered cutting-edge technology. Since this time, the explosion of new music technologies has provided many options that might be employed in clinical situations similar to David's in order to increase the choices for engagement in a music collage process that facilitates self-awareness and self-expression. Chapter 12 will identify some of these newer options and their applications.

Literature Illustrating Music Collage

Like some of the other method-variations discussed in this book, music collage is significantly underrepresented in the literature even though you might imagine that it is a method-variation that MTs might often choose to offer clients. Similarly, when music collage is mentioned, there is often little elaboration on the MT's thought processes in making this decision or making choices for design and implementation. One case description that is helpful in this regard is offered by Heiderscheit, Marmor, Saindon, and

Wellstone (2016), who write about collaborative therapy work in an eating disorder treatment setting.

The clients in this case were an outpatient group for whom the process of creating personal music collages, which they called "songscaped life stories," was offered by the MT to help them to explore their lives in a way that separated their eating disorder from their primary sense of identity. The authors begin the case by outlining the various benefits of narrating one's own life story and discussing how stories and songs can serve as a means of ritual and healing. In particular, this type of music collage allows individuals the chance to recognize dominant themes in their lives, understand and explain those themes, and consider whether they want to continue playing these themes out. Recognizing unhealthy or dysfunctional themes opens the possibility of making different choices in the future.

The authors provide the step-by-step process that they followed to assist the group members in creating their own songscaped life stories and using them as a means of exploring patterns in their lives. This included identifying significant moments in life, selecting songs that represent these moments, arranging them in a playlist format, and writing a summary for each song about how it relates to the corresponding significant moment. The songscaped life stories created by each of the group members were then shared within the group. Significant time was spent listening to each person's collage so that each had the opportunity to learn both from their own story and from the aspects of others' stories that resonated with their own experience. Discussion focused on the themes that were discovered within each story and how those themes might also be similar to others' experiences. An example of the value of this process in one group member's life is also shared within this chapter.

A case discussing the use of music collage with a woman with bipolar disorder (Jackson, 2018a) also provides some insight into the question of clinical decision-making. The client in this case was a woman who had been misdiagnosed for years, resulting in a chronic and difficult-to-manage presentation of bipolar disorder. She had been hospitalized repeatedly with bouts of psychosis and periodic suicidal ideation and attempts, and her low-level chronic paranoia made it difficult for her to trust the professionals who provided treatment in the hospital. The MT began treatment with a receptive method-variation involving preferred music listening in order to build trust. As they listened together, the MT recognized that the client was relating music she chose to specific times and events in her life, and the MT understood this as a means of moving the client into a more self-reflective process in therapy. She suggested that the client make an "album" of music that reflected the important events in her life up to the present, and the client agreed.

During this process, the client's focus for the album began to center strongly around a traumatic time from her youth, and the MT encouraged her to select music to explore this event in depth. As a part of this process, they not only worked with prerecorded music but also recorded some of the client's improvisational explorations of this time that captured her emotions about it and provided her with material for looking at the event from different perspectives. Her improvisations included instrumental improvisation, some of which included vocalization, and others that shifted into song improvisation. Developing the collage process in this way afforded the client the chance to explore her thoughts and feelings more freely in relation to this traumatic experience.

Through the process, the MT helped the client to redefine the "plan" for her autobiographical collage, focusing on the traumatic event with a timeline of before, during, after, and now. She assisted the client in selecting pieces of prerecorded music, recordings of the client's own music-making, and some sampled sounds that the client had identified as descriptive of her feelings and emotions. They worked together to combine these into a unified whole that the client felt represented her timeline around the event. In addition, throughout the process, the MT asked her to make visual representations of her thoughts and feelings and offered her oil pastels and paper. This was particularly helpful in instances during which the client had "played her feelings out" but had still been unprepared to talk about them verbally. The art and words that the client created on paper were combined with her music and sound compilations to create a multimedia autobiography. By its completion, the client improvised music about and verbalized having decided to let this trauma go and to no longer allow it to interfere with her here-and-now. This was reflected in the ending of her music collage.

This case demonstrates adaptations made by the MT to meet the client's level of ability to be challenged at different times in the process, as well as decisions she made to further develop the client's therapeutic exploration. It also represents an experience-based approach to this method-variation. The MT did not plan ahead of time to address trauma with the client, and she did not identify objectives related to this for her treatment process within music therapy. Instead, she allowed the affordances of music to assist the growth of their therapeutic relationship and to reveal what was most pressing for the client in relation to her mental health and well-being. The music collage process naturally brought up the memories, thoughts, and feelings that were most pertinent to the client's emotional health at this time, and the MT's structuring of the process over time simultaneously maintained a safe container for dealing with that traumatic experience and encouraged ever deeper exploration in order to finally arrive at a resolution.

Amir (2012) utilized music collage in a form she calls "musical presentation" to explore and share identity within music therapy group sessions. Musical presentation involves an individual selecting pieces of music that reflect something important about themselves and arranging them in a particular order. They then share the presentation with the rest of the group by playing them and listening together. Amir outlines a number of ways to focus musical presentation, including developmental presentation, historical presentation, presentation of what is in the present, and preference presentation. She also offers specific information about the steps involved in the selection, design, and implementation of musical presentation and various means of analyzing the content, which gives the article strong utilitarian value if you are interested in learning more about this approach to music collage. This information is clarified and further illustrated through the case of Daniella, a music therapy student who explored identity as a part of her music therapy training.

Much as with some other method-variations in this book, literature on music collage within sessions, and in particular from the perspective of the MT and their thought processes for choosing, designing, and implementing music collage, is sparse at best. There is an occasional reference to music autobiography but typically no extrapolation on its use. For example, in a chapter by Heiderscheit (2013) on the use of the Bonny Method of Guided

Imagery and Music (GIM) model in eating disorder treatment, she mentions that music biography was selected to engage the client in this case until she was strong enough and had stabilized her cognitive functioning enough to meet the prerequisite demands of GIM work. This suggests that the adaptable nature of music collage was useful in meeting the client's needs for a time, but because music collage was not the focus of the chapter, no other information about the design and implementation of music biography is offered.

Other Literature Related to Music Collage

A community-based research project by Gilboa, Yehuda, and Amir (2009) utilized Amir's musical presentation experience to increase understanding between group members of differing cultures of origin, in this case a group of students composed of some who were Israeli-born and some who were immigrants resettled in Israel. The researchers made clear that this project did not involve music therapy, but they did make use of the affordances of musical presentation in service of assisting the participants in the acceptance and appreciation of those who were different from themselves. The data taken from the group suggested that this approach helped participants to have greater identification with their own cultural roots as well as develop more openness and acceptance of others. The fact that this study did not involve the use of music as part of treatment underscores that the affordances of music are not relegated to individuals experiencing it as treatment but are affordances of all human beings who engage in music. While the sharing of a music collage affords treatment-related experiences to the music therapy client because of the opportunities created by the MT, we all can experience the benefit of sharing who we are and what we value when we share our chosen music.

An excellent example of a playlist-formatted music collage is the new book entitled *Music Is History* (Questlove, 2021). This book is a musical autobiography in which the author selects a song for each year of his life based on its meaning to him and the societal, cultural, and historical contexts it reflects. While it is only in written verbal form (to listen you must find the audio recordings yourself) and it is not the product of a formal therapy process, it captures the spirit of how music embodies and communicates something of meaning about the person who selects and combines it in an intentional manner. Questlove is known for curating playlists for people, each of which is focused on some aspect related to the individual for whom it was created. If you are interested in expanding the way you think about music collage as a means of engagement in therapy, you might find this book to be revelatory and valuable.

The *Guidelines for Music Therapy Practice* series from Barcelona, again, offers information about selecting, designing, and implementing music collage experiences in a variety of settings and with clients with a broad range of therapeutic needs. You will want to use these resources to help you in your thought processes relative to your clinical setting. Music collage is not addressed as frequently in these volumes as other method-variations might be, but you will still find a good array of application, from the use of music collage to help children who are undergoing treatment for severe burns to tell their stories and explore their feelings (Whitehead-Pleaux (2014) to the creation of playlists to address mood states (Eyre, 2014a) to the use of musical autobiography for life review in palliative care (Clements-Cortés, 2014). The tables that follow list all of the chapters that address music collage, arranged by volume.

Table 11.0
Guidelines for Music Therapy Practice in Mental Health
(Eyre, 2014b)

Author	Chapter	Title
Eyre	4	Adults in a Recovery Model Setting
Zanders	6	Foster Care Youth
Jackson	11	Adults with Depression and/or Anxiety
Murphy	14	Adults with Substance Use Disorders
McFerran	15	Adolescents with Substance Use Disorders
Hatcher	9	Adult Male Survivors of Abuse and Developmental Trauma
Jackson	11	Adults with Depression and/or Anxiety
Dvorkin	12	Adults and Adolescents with Borderline Personality Disorder
Murphy	14	Adults with Substance Use Disorders

McFerran	15	Adolescents with Substance Use Disorders
Rea-Kolb	19	Juvenile Male Sex Offenders
Young	21	Persons with Alzheimer's Disease and Other Dementias
Gardstrom	18	Adjudicated Adolescents
Rea-Kolb	19	Juvenile Male Sex Offenders
Young	21	Persons with Alzheimer's Disease and Other Dementias

Table 11.1
Guidelines for Music Therapy Practice in Pediatric Care
(Bradt, 2014)

Author	Chapter	Title
Ghetti	5	Pediatric Intensive Care
Whitehead-Pleaux	7	Burn Care for Children
Dun	8	Children with Cancer
Neugebauer	13	Children in General Inpatient Care

Table 11.2
Guidelines for Music Therapy Practice in Adult Medical Care
(Allen, 2014)

Author	Chapter	Title
Clements-Cortez	12	Adults in Palliative/Hospice Care
Daveson	13	Caring for Caregivers

References

Allen, J. (2014). *Guidelines for music therapy practice in adult medical care*. Barcelona Publishers.

Amir, D. (2012). "My music is me": Musical presentation as a way of forming and sharing identity in music therapy group. *Nordic Journal of Music Therapy, 21*(2), 176–193. http://dx.doi.org/10.1080/08098131.2011.571279

Bradt, J. (2014). *Guidelines for music therapy practice in pediatric care*. Barcelona Publishers.

Clements-Cortés, A. (2014). Adults in palliative care and hospice. In J. Allen (Ed.), *Guidelines for music therapy practice in adult medical care* (pp. 295–346). Barcelona Publishers.

Eyre, L. (2014a). Adults in a recovery model setting. In L. Eyre (Ed.), *Guidelines for music therapy practice in mental health* (pp. 115–167). Barcelona Publishers.

Eyre, L. (2014b). *Guidelines for music therapy practice in mental health.* Barcelona Publishers.

Gilboa, A., Yehuda, N., & Amir, D. (2009). Let's talk music: A musical-communal project for enhancing communication among students of multicultural origin. *Nordic Journal of Music Therapy, 18*(1), 3–31. doi:10.1080/08098130802610999

Heiderscheit, A. (2016). GIM: Deprivation and its contribution to pain in eating disorders. In J. F. Mondanaro & G. A. Sara (Eds.), *Music and medicine: Integrative models in the treatment of pain* (pp. 347–372). Satchnote Press.

Heiderscheit, A., & Jackson, N. (2018). *Introduction to music therapy practice.* Barcelona Publishers.

Heiderscheit, A., Marmor, T. M., Saindon, S., & Wellstone, L. (2016). Collaborating with a creative arts therapist. In A. Heiderscheit (Ed.), *Creative arts therapies and clients with eating disorders* (pp. 357–376). Jessica Kingsley.

Jackson, N. (2018a). Case C3—Autobiographical collage with a woman with bipolar disorder. In A. Heiderscheit & N. Jackson, *Introduction to music therapy practice* (pp. 163–167). Barcelona Publishers.

Jackson, N. (2018b). Case C4—Multimedia composition with a man with developmental disability. In A. Heiderscheit & N. Jackson, *Introduction to music therapy practice* (pp. 170–172). Barcelona Publishers.

Questlove (2021). *Music is history.* Abrams Image.

Whitehead-Pleaux, A. (2014). Burn care for children. In J. Bradt (Ed.), *Guidelines for music therapy practice in pediatric care* (pp. 252–289). Barcelona Publishers.

12

USE OF TECHNOLOGY IN COMPOSITIONAL METHODS

Overview of Technology in Compositional Method-variations

Technology plays a key role in compositional methods. Developments and advancements in technology provide applications, tools, and resources that allow MTs to support and engage clients in the composition and music production process in new and different ways. Technology may be integrated at different stages, utilized throughout, and used in various ways in the composition process. The ways in which technology is implemented into the therapeutic process are influenced by the needs and preferences of the client, the method-variation, the music genre, and whether/how the composition is recorded.

This chapter is designed to help to explore the considerations for the client or group in making decisions about the technology that will help to facilitate music making and make it accessible, as well as to support and engage clients in the compositional process. The chapter provides several clinical case illustrations focused on technology considerations relevant to the client or group. You will discover that your creativity and critical thinking skills are important assets in this process as you explore the possibilities and ways in which technology can be a valuable tool to engage your clients in compositional methods.

It is helpful to begin by identifying the basic considerations for the uses of technology with compositional method-variations. These can be explored through the following questions:

- What is the sound source for the composition?
- How will I record or capture the composition?
- How will I store the composition?
- How will I disseminate the composition?

These questions will help you to begin to determine the technology that will best serve the needs of your client or group, as well as the compositional method-variation. The sound source may include voice, piano, guitar, or any other instrumentation, and the composition may integrate multiple sound or media sources. Determining the sound source and what, if any, mixed media may be utilized will then help you to begin to decide how to record the composition. Following the completion of the recording, you will need to identify where, how, and how long the composition will be stored. Last, you will need to consider how you will disseminate the recording of the composition to the client or group of clients. This will include understanding the format in which you need to provide their recording for it to be accessible. An important consideration in this process is protecting the privacy and confidentiality of the clients. These considerations will be discussed more fully later in the chapter. Figure 12.0 illustrates a basic signal flow, showing how the music created is picked up, recorded, listened to, and shared.

Figure 12.0. Illustration of basic signal flow. In the basic signal flow, there are one or more sound sources (such as a guitar) that are picked up through a microphone and recorded on a device (such as a tablet or laptop). The therapist and client(s) can then listen to the recording, which may be shared if appropriate.

Clinical Technology Case Illustrations

The clinical technology cases provide illustrations of various compositional method-variations in different clinical contexts. The cases included in this section focus on different technology tools and resources that you may use in the composition process with clients. Each case explores a different clinical context and scenario focused on technology considerations for the composition process. Questions and considerations specific to each case are included to help you to begin to identify different and unique considerations for individual or group songwriting and multi- and mixed media compositions. Each case illustration includes two technology diagrams to demonstrate different options you can choose and utilize. Keep in mind that these are not the only two options but simply the two options provided. As new technology develops, there will continually be new resources and tools available for use. The process of identifying your considerations will help to guide you in your decision-making about which technologies will best meet the needs of each composition project.

Clinical Technology Case One

In Chapter 7, we presented a case that included a group of adolescents in an inpatient mental health unit who were engaged in group songwriting. Their song focused on their struggles with alcohol and drug use, as well as suicidal and homicidal thoughts. The group decided collectively to structure and record their song in rap form. After the group had made the decisions about genre and to record their rap, there were considerations related to the technology. For their rap, the group selected the rhythm and beats from different options available on a drum machine. The drum machine had a speaker so that the rhythms generated were audible to the group as they rapped their lyrics and recorded the composition. Recording a song that a group has composed can present many different considerations for an MT. To determine your technology needs, it may be helpful to consider the following: What equipment or technology is available for use in creating and recording the song?

- What technology is accessible to the client(s)?
- What technology supports the genre or style of the composition?
- Are you recording a group singing simultaneously?
- Are you recording individuals of the group singing alternatively?
- Do you need to record multiple tracks and then mix them?
- How will you store the recording?
- In what format do you need the composition in order to distribute it to the group?
- Are the devices you are using for recording HIPAA-compliant? (i.e., institutional and not personal devices)

The answers to these questions will help you to determine the technology you might utilize to record the group composition. To help you to understand how recording a group composition may occur in different ways, two technology illustrations are included based on Clinical Technology Case One. The group composed their piece in rap form. They decided to use a drum machine to generate the beats for their song, to which group members would alternate in singing the lyrics. Figure 12.1 demonstrates the technology flow based on these considerations and decisions.

Figure 12.1. Technology illustration. The clients utilize a drum machine to provide the rhythm for their rap. The combined sounds of their voices and the drum machine are picked up by the microphone and recorded onto a laptop. The group listens to the recording of their rap.

Figure 12.2 provides you with an alternative to consider if the group makes different decisions regarding how they want to record their song. If the group decides they want to be able to make more decisions about the rhythms and beats for their rap, GarageBand may be a better alternative to allow them to have more control over the musical elements of their composition. The group may decide they want to rap together, so you need to capture several people singing simultaneously. This configuration will impact the equipment you use to record.

Figure 12.2. Technology illustration. The clients utilize a beat-making app on a tablet to provide the rhythm for their rap. Their voices are picked up by the microphone and recorded onto the tablet, where tracks can be edited and mixed. The group then listens to the recording of their rap, which can be shared as an MP3.

Clinical Technology Case Two

Chapter 11 included a case utilizing a music collage with David, a 26-year-old man with neurodevelopmental disabilities. The MT engaged David in selecting songs and excerpts of songs from the albums in the music room that he wanted to be included in his music collage, creating drawings that represented how the music made him feel, and choosing artwork from existing album covers. The MT played the LP record on a turntable and connected it to the computer to digitize David's song selections and then the songs were burned onto a CD. The artwork that David created was reduced in size using a copy machine and inserted in the CD case as the album cover.

When creating a music collage and utilizing multi or mixed media there are several considerations related to the origins of the song source, the mix of media, the format the music collage needs to be in to give to the client.

- What is the format of the songs or song excerpts?
- Do the songs need to be moved to a different format for use? Are excerpts of songs needed for the project? Does the process require splicing to capture song segments or excerpts?
- What types of media are being integrated?

- Does the project require video?
- Are visual components or original artwork included in the music collage?
- What technology is needed to capture visual or artwork images for the project?
- What is the appropriate format for storing the music collage?
- What is the format needed to provide the music collage to the client?

Determining the answers to these questions helps you to identify which technology tools and resources to use for a client's music collage. You may need to talk with the client and ask what their preferences are about the media they want to use and the format they want for their music collage. In this case, the songs available at the treatment facility were in LP format and needed to be recorded on the computer to be digitized. Figure 12.3 illustrates the technology flow for this process.

Figure 12.3. Technology illustration. The vinyl records are played on the turntable connected by USB to the laptop. The laptop records the music in digital form. The songs are then copied onto a CD that is given to the client.

Clinical Technology Case Three

Lucy was a 1-month-old patient in the Pediatric Intensive Care Unit (PICU). She had been diagnosed with a rare life-threatening disease called Transthyretin Amyloid Cardiomyopathy (ATTR-CM), which causes a buildup of protein in the heart that leads to progressive heart failure. Lucy and her family (Mom, Dad, and 3-year-old brother Jack) participated in family music therapy sessions. The sessions were focused on fostering their relationships and connection as a family through music because this was a medium they could share even while Lucy was hospitalized. When the medical team informed Lucy's parents that the progression of the disease had caused such significant damage that there was nothing more they could do, they wanted to focus the music therapy sessions on making memories as a family. One of the ways in which they did this was to create a song as a family, engaging Jack and Lucy in the process as they were able to participate. Lucy's mom and dad worked with the MT to write the words to their song, expressing their thoughts and feelings about their family, their children, and how much they loved each other. Jack was given spots in the song to fill in blanks with his thoughts and feelings. Since Lucy was still nonverbal, the MT suggested recording her giggles and heartbeat to integrate into the family song. Her parents were thrilled with the idea of capturing Lucy's sounds so that her presence could be included in the song.

    The MT utilized a microphone connected to a laptop to record Lucy's giggles in GarageBand. Lucy smiled and giggled when she was with her family and responding to their voices and expressions. Their interactions and her giggles were put into a track in GarageBand. Mom, Dad, and Jack sang their song, accompanied by the MT on guitar. This was also recorded by a microphone as the family gathered around and recorded into GarageBand. Lucy's heartbeat was recorded using an Eko digital stethoscope. The MT worked with Lucy's nurse to capture the recording of Lucy's heartbeat. The Eko stethoscope has Bluetooth capabilities, so it recorded the heartbeat and sent the recording to an app on the MT's iPad. The recording was then converted and put into GarageBand on the laptop. The MT was then able to mix the three tracks into a single recording to create the family's song, which was then given to the family as an MP3 recording that became a keepsake that they could share with extended family members. Figure 12.4 illustrates the two different recording processes needed to create the tracks that were then mixed.

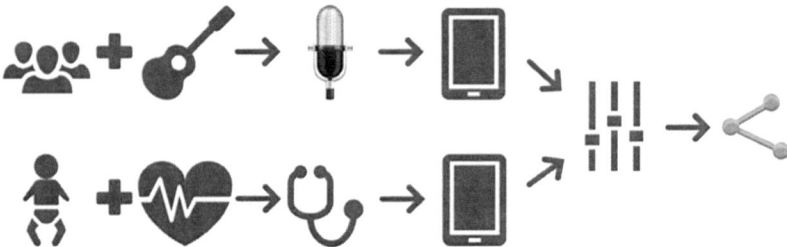

Figure 12.4. Technology illustration. The family sings their song, accompanied by the MT on guitar. Their voices and the accompaniment are picked up through the microphone and recorded on a tablet. Another recording is made by using the Eko digital stethoscope to pick up the infant's heartbeat. This recording is sent via Bluetooth to the tablet. The two recordings are then edited and mixed and shared with the family as an MP3.

Technology to Assist Client Engagement

There is a wide array of different types of technology that can be implemented and utilized in the composition process to provide assistance that clients may need for engaging in these various aspects of the composition process. Assistive technology is intended to increase, maintain, or improve a client's capabilities. Integrating devices and applications that foster a client's engagement in the composition process provides the opportunity for them to feel empowered in the therapeutic process and feel a greater sense of ownership of their composition. It is important to understand what assistance and support the client may need in order to identify and determine which assistive and adaptive technologies will be appropriate and most helpful. The following questions will help you to determine the considerations relevant to a client or group:

- What type of assistance does the client need to foster and support engagement?
    - Physical
    - Expressive communication
    - Social interaction
    - Independent functioning
    - Music creation

- In which part of the composition process does the client need assistance in engaging?
    - Expressing and communicating ideas for song lyrics or music
    - Creating the song lyrics
    - Playing and sharing their ideas for the music
    - Playing their music for recording
    - Playing their music live for others

- What technology do I have that can support the client's engagement?

- What technology does the client have that might support their engagement?

- Can any of the assistive or adaptive devices that are currently accessible be modified to meet the client's needs?

- Are there assistive or adaptive devices that may need to be purchased to support the client's engagement?

- Are there applications that may support the client's engagement?

- What is the level of technical skill the client possesses (low, moderate, or high)?

- Are there any limitations I need to consider regarding technology?
    - Limited access to an outlet to a plug-in
    - The device cannot be cleaned with cleaner or wipes required for contact precautions
    - Client mobility or positioning

Assistive technologies are applications, equipment, devices, tools, and resources that can be purchased commercially and are available free for use or are adapted, modified, or even customized. Table 12.0 identifies several different assistive or adaptive devices and applications that may be useful in supporting and engaging clients in communication during the composition process, as well as in creating and recording compositions. The table provides a brief description of different devices and applications and information on how the device or application can be helpful to clients. While this table provides an introduction to technology that can be useful in the composition process, it is not intended to represent all available technology resources or what may best serve the unique needs of your client.

Table 12.0
Assistive and Adaptive Devices

Assistive or Adaptive Device or Application	Description of Device or Application	How It Can Be Helpful
Visual representation systems	Software or applications that include photographs, realistic drawings, images, or words	Allow the client to select pictures, images, or words that represent what they want to communicate in the composition process or images that they want to be included as a part of their music collage
Voice output communication aids	A device that is paired with visual images that allow the client to push a button and express what they want to communicate	Supports the client in expressive communication, as they can operate the buttons of the device to foster their expressive communication
Adaptive switches	A switch that allows the user to activate assistive technology devices	Allows a client with a physical limitation or communication need to press the button and activate a communication or mobile device, environmental controls, or computer software
Beams	A touch-free device that uses sensor technology to translate movement into sound and music	Senses the movement made by the client and creates music and/or sound based on the movement
Virtual guitar	An application that allows the user to see and hear chords and scales on the guitar fretboard	Engages the client in selecting chord or scale options from any key and play in the key of their choice

Virtual instruments	Applications available and accessible on mobile devices that can be utilized	Provides options for various virtual instruments, with free and purchase applications; allows the client to select and play the instrument
MIDI controllers	Device or application that the client can manipulate through subtle movement or breath(ring, breath, IOS app)	Allows the client to control any aspect of a software instrument (e.g., dynamics, volume, vibrato, etc.)

Clinical Technology Case Four

Zachary was 9 years old and had been diagnosed with autism. He was able to participate in the classroom with peers of the same age but struggled socially and emotionally at school and home much of the time. Zachary demonstrated advanced skills with technology (iPad), memorization, and math. Parents sought music therapy for Zachary to help to address his anger, inappropriate behaviors (hitting and yelling), and rigid thinking, as well as for learning and developing social skills. One of the first needs addressed in the music therapy sessions focused on developing social skills. This was facilitated by the MT utilizing two iPads (Zachary's and the MT's) to create vocal and instrumental compositions. Virtual instruments in GarageBand supported Zachary's engagement, as he could choose and make decisions about the various digital instruments and sounds he wanted to include in the orchestra of his composition. This involved Zachary choosing the virtual instruments he would play and those that the MT would play. Individual tracks were recorded of various virtual instruments. These tracks were then mixed in GarageBand and after Zachary and the MT listened to the complete composition. After the composition was listened to and discussed, the composition was deleted. This allowed Zachary to move on to the next composition without an attachment to the previous one or focusing on comparing his two compositions. Instead, he could enjoy the temporary nature of his creation and the experience, which then enabled him to transition more easily to each successive song. Figure 12.5 illustrates the technology flow utilized to create and record Zachary's composition.

Figure 12.5. Technology illustration. The client's singing is picked up through a microphone and recorded on a tablet. Using a sampling app, the client's recorded voice is used as the pitches of an electronic instrument, which then can be played on the tablet to create a composition. The client can then listen to the composition that has been created.

Figure 12.6. Technology illustration. The MT and client each use their own tablets with electronic instrument apps, which are synced to one another, to create a composition together. When it is completed, they listen to their recorded composition.

Clinical Technology Case Five

Martin was 74 years old and had lived alone since his wife had died 3 years previously. He had had a quadruple bypass that had successfully removed the significant blockage. He had struggled with asthma since childhood and found that singing was a helpful way to improve his breathing. He sang in a community choir and had weekly music therapy sessions to engage him in singing to help to manage his asthma. Martin engaged in singing his favorite songs and oftentimes enjoyed replacing the original lyrics with his own to personalize the song in some way. This led the MT to introduce the idea of song composition because Martin often enjoyed creating his own lyrics. This sparked Martin's idea to write a song for each of his children and grandchildren. After composing all of the songs, he recorded them and included all eight songs on a CD that he gave to each of his children and grandchildren. This album allowed him to create an original song that expressed his feelings about each of them, to share his hopes and dreams for them, and to record himself singing their songs.

Martin's music therapy sessions occurred in two different formats, face-to-face and virtual (telecommunications). Since Martin no longer drove beyond his immediate neighborhood due to concerns that his family had about driving in the city, he was dependent on extended family for transportation to music therapy sessions. In the weeks when he did not have a ride, Martin and the MT were able to meet via a telecommunications platform. Martin regularly used his computer to remain in contact with his family through email and Zoom calls, so he was able to easily engage with the platform for music therapy sessions. Being able to have his sessions in both formats and using technology to support this ensured that Martin was able to meet consistently with the MT and not experience disruption in his therapeutic progress.

Figure 12.7 illustrates the signal flow utilized during Martin's face-to-face music therapy sessions to play and record his songs. Figure 12.8 illustrates the technology and signal flow during his telehealth music therapy sessions.

Figure 12.7. Technology illustration. Utilizing a Bluetooth MIDI keyboard connected to a tablet with a music recording app, the client and MT created the accompaniment tracks for each of the song compositions and then listened to each track.

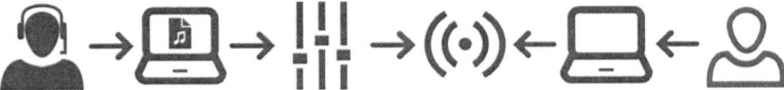

Figure 12.8. Technology illustration. Due to the need to meet via telehealth for the next session, the MT and the client each logged onto their laptop to join a video call. The client and MT listened to recordings from the previous in-person session and then made decisions and edited the tracks to finalize their accompaniment recordings.

Technology and Ethical Considerations

The accessibility and ease with which we can engage technology is an asset in clinical practice. These various devices allow MTs, clients, and their family members to use personal mobile devices to capture audio and video recordings. This also raises important considerations regarding the implications of this access. While MTs may have their own personal mobile devices that can be used for recording client compositions, your personal devices shouldn't be utilized to capture a client's composition. While the device is password-protected, this still could lead to the recording being inadvertently viewed or shared, which would be a violation of the Health Insurance Portability and Accountability Act (HIPAA) (Cohen & Mello, 2018). The best practice is to have a mobile device (iPad, laptop, etc.) that is purchased by the clinical site and dedicated for use in music therapy sessions.

Clients who choose to create recordings of their composition may wish to share their creation with family and loved ones. While the client has the right to choose with whom they wish to share their recording, it will be important to know in which format they want or need their composition in order to share it with others. If you want to use the client's recording in a presentation or on the organization's social media platform, you will need to get a signed consent from the client and/or a parent/guardian (depending on the age of the client). A client's composition can be a very personal and intimate artifact of their therapeutic work, and, as a result, they need to decide whether they want this shared with others.

Compositions created by groups also carry important considerations when members of the group are provided with a recording of their composition, which should not include any information that can reveal any of the clients' identities (e.g., names). If a copy of the recording is being provided to the clients, you will need to determine the format for the artifact and how it will be given to each client. It is also helpful to have the group discuss with whom they are comfortable in having their composition shared in order to be respectful of each other's privacy. Additionally, if you want to include the group's composition in a presentation to staff or at a professional conference, you must obtain permission from each member of the group and have documented consent. As a professional, this ensures you are abiding by the ethical standards of practice (AMTA, 2019) and protecting the clients' privacy. While issues related to technology are addressed only minimally in the AMTA Code of Ethics, the document does provide guidance on ways to address ethical issues as they may relate to social media platforms. Bates (2014) explores this explicitly to avoid errors related to the use of technology in music therapy practice and recommends being aware of ethical implications relevant to the technology being utilized and of how to maintain HIPAA compliance and remain informed as technology changes.

Considerations for Selecting Technology for Your Music Therapy Practice

There are a myriad of applications, devices, and types of technology that can be useful when engaging clients in compositional method-variations. There are applications you may be able to access that are free, while others are available for a fee. There are many devices, equipment, software programs, and tools that can range in capabilities and cost. This may feel overwhelming as you consider all of the possibilities available and even challenging when trying to determine what will best meet the needs of your clients. It is helpful to consider that there may not be one right answer but instead various options from which to choose. Similar to the critical thinking skills you have learned when making clinical decisions about the method-variations, these same skills are imperative when you are making decisions about the technology needed for your clinical practice. There are several questions and considerations that can help to guide your decision-making process:

- What are the functions needed? (Audio and/or video recording?)
- What is the budget available for technology?
- Are there applications that may be free?
- Is there technology already available at the clinical site that can be utilized?
- Are there infection control policies that may impact technology decisions?
- Can the equipment be wiped and sanitized?
- Is the technology or application secure enough to protect the client's privacy?
- Does this technology or equipment serve multiple functions?
- What are the benefits this technology offers?
- What are the limitations of this technology?
- Are these different technologies compatible?
- Is there technology needed to support client engagement?
    - If so, what type of support is needed?
    - Does the client already have technology that may be useful?

There may be additional questions that arise as you explore how to support a client's engagement in compositional method-variations. These questions can be unique to the clinical setting or the needs and preferences of the clients. It can also be helpful to consult other music therapists to find out what technologies they are using and find most effective. Their experience can provide answers and insights that you may not have considered.

The Changing Nature of Technology

The rapid changes in technology continue to transform our world. As MTs, we must continue to educate ourselves to stay informed about technologies that may benefit our clients, foster accessibility, support engagement, and enhance service delivery. There are a variety of ways in which you can stay informed about new and emerging technologies that may be appropriate for use with compositional method-variations.

- Talk to and consult with other MTs about what they are using
- Talk to colleagues in other disciplines

- Talk to the client, parent, or guardian to inquire whether there is new technology they are using at home or school
- Join social media groups of professionals working in similar clinical settings or client populations
    - Review the literature
    - Music therapy literature
- Related literature
- Learn about new technology and applications at conferences
    - Workshops
    - Vendors in exhibit halls

It is helpful to remember that people are resources and that you can learn about new and different technologies as you consult with music therapy colleagues and other professionals. Additionally, the music therapy body of literature exploring the use of technology is growing and will continue to increase exponentially as MTs discover new and different ways that benefit clients and can be integrated into clinical practice.

Review of Literature on Technology for Compositional Method-variations

The breadth of technology available and accessible for music therapy practice continues to grow and is being utilized in a myriad of clinical settings with clients across the life span. The review of the literature included here provides a brief overview as it relates to the use of technology with compositional method-variations. Exploring the literature surrounding the integration of technologies into this facet of music therapy practice demonstrates the many different types of technology that can be useful. This can range from computer software, mobile devices, applications, switches, beams, and amplification equipment to devices that use musical instrument digital interface (MIDI) technology (Hahna et al., 2012). Also addressed are the challenges that MTs face in using these tools.

These tools can foster communication, enable emotional expression, compensate for physical limitations, empower a client and increase their autonomy, and serve as a means of motivation (Magee, 2011). Technology and applications also give clients access to a wider variety of instrumentation and timbres (Magee &

Burland, 2008a) for use in compositional method-variations. It is helpful to review the literature in order to better understand the general benefits and limitations involved when implementing music technology (Magee & Burland, 2008b; Partesotti, Peñalba, & Manzolli, 2018) and to understand how these apply to the song and music composition process. Knight and Lagasse (2012) explore advances in music technologies and provide a review of various applications related to their use in music therapy practice. Knight and Krout (2017) examine four different categories of music technologies and provide evaluations of them to assist clinicians in understanding efficiently and effectively the potential of these applications.

The literature illustrates the many different goal areas that different technologies can address, as well as the specific technology tool or resource that is most suitable to address the respective goal (Werger, Groothuis, & Jaschke, 2020). More recently, the literature is examining the use of technology to support engagement in music therapy sessions through telehealth communication platforms (Agres, Foubert, & Sridhar, 2021). The integration of various technology tools warrants consideration of the role that technology plays in the creation and co-creation process. Jonassen (2021) explores how to approach the integration of technology into the therapeutic process and suggests seeing these tools as co-agents. Additionally, Krüger (2007) encourages MTs to examine their own relationship with music and technology to better understand how they can collaboratively meet the needs of the client.

While the body of literature on the use of compositional method-variations is robust, much of the literature focuses on describing the therapeutic process rather than the integration of technology in the creation, recording, or performance of the composition. The literature related to the use of technology is growing. Table 12.1 includes a brief description of each case and provides details about the technologies explored and utilized in each case. Citations are also included to provide the information if you want to access the full article or book chapter.

Table 12.1
Case Examples in the Literature of the Use of Technology with Compositional Method-variations

Description of Case	Focus of Case	Reference
Use of alternative modes of communication in the song composition process	Considerations and recommendations when using alternative methods of communication with clients with traumatic brain injuries in the songwriting process	Baker, 2005
Descriptions of technology utilized in song composition process within a hospital setting	Details about basic signal flow and the technology utilized in recording songs created by pediatric patients are illustrated in several case examples; discussion of limitations and recommendations for technology	Aasgaard, 2005
Songwriting with an adolescent diagnosed with muscular dystrophy	Clinical case reviewing 19-session series with an adolescent male living with muscular dystrophy; exploration of the use of the sound beam to support his engagement in actively creating the music	Dwyer, 2007
Use of telecommunication technology in the collaborative songwriting process	Music therapy students' use of telecommunication technology to collaborate with peers in songwriting experience	Krout, Baker, & Muhlberger, 2010
Descriptions of various types of technology that can be implemented to support client engagement	Explanations and illustrations of different technologies and assistive devices to support communication, musical engagement, and creation with clients across the life span; case vignettes were included to demonstrate the role that technology played when implemented for each client	Magee et al., 2011

Descriptions and uses for various iPad applications	Exploration of the various applications and apps available for use on the iPad (free and fee-based) and descriptions of their use in music therapy in creating music and recording songs	Knight, 2013
Exploration of the use of digital workstations in music therapy practice	Descriptions, benefits, and limitations of digital audio workstations (DAW) such as GarageBand, Logic Pro, Ableton Live, and Pro Tools	Sandovnik, 2014; Weissberg, 2014
Focus on the creation of rap music and the various elements of and ways to approach the composition process and mixing these elements	Descriptions and illustrations of technology used in creating compositions, including rapping over precomposed music, melodies, and beats and mixing tracks	Baker, 2015
The role of technology in creating the music for song compositions	Explanations of the different ways in which software technology can shape the music (loops, layering, distorting, adding reverb, recording, and mixing); brief case examples describing the use of the technology to support the therapeutic process	Baker, 2015
Descriptions of compositional method-variations that integrate portions or elements of different songs	Descriptions of techniques of mash-up, pastiche, and hodge-podge and the technology utilized in the process of creating the composition; various case illustrations are included that describe how technology is utilized	Baker, 2015
Exploration of computer technology that can be utilized in composition-based interventions	Descriptions of how computer technology can support and foster interactive processes	Johnston, Egerman, & Kearney, 2018

Heartbeat recording integrated with song composition in perinatal palliative care and with parents and children with neurodegenerative illnesses	Case illustrations of song compositions by families that integrate the heartbeat recording of their infant and themes that emerged in their process	Andrews et al., 2020; Schreck & Economos, 2018; Walden et al., 2021
Video recording of adolescent transplant patient's song	The case provides a brief description of the recording process, the process of giving the recording to the patient, and the response to the patient's request to share the video recording with her surgeon and hospital's social media page	Heiderscheit, 2018
Contextualization of music technology within the hip-hop tradition of beat-making	A brief historical account about the origins of the beat-making tradition in hip-hop culture; descriptions of beats and technology and their relevance and application in music therapy practice	Crooke, 2018
Exploration of songwriting with adolescents and the use of technology in digital layering	Discussion of the role that technology plays in songwriting with adolescents who have experienced trauma and various recording and production techniques and their clinical function	Viega, 2018
Technology-based group therapeutic songwriting with clients with muscular dystrophy	Exploration of a group of clients with physical limitations and how technology was utilized to support their composition process with music software, MIDI keyboard, drum machines, loops, and an audio interface	Edgar, Tsiris, & Rickson, 2019
Visual supports utilized in music therapy sessions to foster communication	Examples of various types of augmentative and alternative communication utilized for visual support and	Fuller & Short, 2020

descriptions of why MTs use them in sessions

Other valuable resources for further delving into the use of technology are the books *Music Technology in Therapeutic and Health Settings* (Magee, 2014) and *Music, Health, Technology, and Design* (Stensæth, 2014). These books provide a background and overview of the use of technology in various clinical settings, an introduction to assistive devices, and indications and contra-indications regarding the use of technology. The chapters explore different types of technology with clients of various ages and therapeutic needs and explore future directions of music technology. While the text is focused on music technology, it is not limited to compositional method-variations; still, it can serve as a valuable resource as you consider and explore technology for use with these method-variations. Another useful text is *Therapeutic songwriting: Developments in theory, methods, and practice* (Baker, 2015). This text provides a comprehensive overview of songwriting and includes specific information related to the use of technology in the composition process. Magee and Stensæth (2016) explore the history, evolution, and current practices regarding the use of technology in music therapy practice. They also explore ways in which music therapists can collaborate with various interdisciplinary professionals to foster and support the use of technology in their work.

The body of literature related to the use of technology with compositional methods will continue to grow as MTs continue to integrate new and different technologies into their clinical work. It is important to recognize that what is represented in the literature does not give a complete picture of all of the technology that is currently being utilized in practice or of all the ways in which these technologies are being utilized. As a result, it is helpful to talk to other music therapists, professionals from other disciplines, and clients regarding the technologies that they are using in their practice. You will also find it helpful to consider the technology you utilize in your life—and in making music—as you think creatively about how these may become resources and tools in the therapeutic context.

References

Aasgaard, T. (2005). Assisting children with malignant blood diseases to create and perform their own songs. In F. Baker & T. Wigram (Eds.), *Songwriting: Methods, techniques, and clinical applications for music therapy clinicians, educators, and students* (pp. 154–179). Jessica Kingsley Publishers.

Aasgaard, T., & Blichfeldt Ærø, S. (2016). Songwriting techniques in music therapy practice. In J. Edwards (Ed.), *The Oxford Handbook of Music Therapy* (pp. 644–668). Oxford University Press.

Agres, K., Foubert, K., & Sridhar, S. (2021). Music therapy during COVID-19: Changes to practice, use of technology, and what to carry forward in the future. *Frontiers in Psychology, 12,* 647790. doi:10.3389/fpsyg.2021.647790

American Music Therapy Association. (2019). *Code of Ethics.* Retrieved August 30, 2021, from www.musictherapy.org

Andrews, E., Hayes, A., Ceruli, L., Miller, E., & Salmon, N. (2020). Legacy-building in pediatric end-of-life care through innovative use of digital stethoscopes. *Palliative Medicine Reports, 1*(1), 149–155. doi:10.1089/pmr.2020.0028

Baker, F. (2005). Working with impairments in pragmatics through songwriting following traumatic brain injury. In F. Baker & T. Wigram (Eds.), *Songwriting: Methods, techniques, and clinical applications for music therapy clinicians, educators, and students* (pp. 134–153). Jessica Kingsley Publishers.

Baker, F. (2015). *Therapeutic songwriting: Developments in theory, methods, and practice.* Palgrave Macmillan.

Cohen, G., & Mello, M. (2018). HIPAA and protecting health information in the 21st century. *Journal of the American Medical Association, 320*(3), 231–232. doi:10.1001/jama.2018.5630

Crooke, A. (2018). Music technology and the hip-hop beat-making tradition: A history and typology of equipment for music therapy. *Voices: A World Forum for Music Therapy, 18*(2). https://doi.org/10.15845/voices.v18i2.996

Dwyer, O. (2007). Would you like to write your own song? Song writing to address the paradox of emerging capabilities and diminishing possibilities experienced by an adolescent boy with Muscular Dystrophy. *Voices: A World Forum for Music Therapy, 7*(2). https://doi.org/10.15845/voices.v7i2.494

Edgar, J., Tsiris, G., & Rickson, D. (2019). The screams crashed into silence: A therapeutic songwriting project for young adults with life-shortening illnesses. In A. Ludwig (Ed.), *Music therapy in children and young people's palliative care* (pp. 159–173). Jessica Kingsley Publishers.

Fuller, A., & Short, A. (2020). The utilisation of visual supports within music therapy practice in Australia: Listening and looking. *Australian Journal of Music Therapy, 31,* 1–27.

Hahna, N., Hadley, S., Miller, V., & Bonaventura, M. (2012). Music technology usage in music therapy: A survey of practice. *The Arts in Psychotherapy, 30,* 456–464. doi:10.1016/j.aip.2012.08.001.

Heiderscheit, A. (2018). Composition to cope with auto-islet total pancreatectomy transplant. In A. Heiderscheit & N. Jackson (Eds.), *Introduction to music therapy practice* (pp. 183–185). Barcelona Publishers.

Johnston, D., Egermann, H., & Kearney, G (2018). Innovative computer technology in music-based interventions for individuals with autism moving beyond traditional interactive music therapy techniques. *Cogent Psychology, 5*(1), 1554773. doi:10.1080/23311908.2018.1554773

Jonassen, K. (2021). Music technology tools—A therapist in a box? Human-computer interaction and the co-creation of mental health. *Voices: A World Forum for Music Therapy, 21*(2). doi:10.15845/voices.v21i2.3308

Knight, A. (2013). Uses of iPad applications in music therapy. *Music Therapy Perspectives, 31*(1), 189–196. doi:10.1093/mtp/31/2/189

Knight, A., & Krout, R. (2017). Making sense of today's electronic music technology: Resources for music therapy. *Music Therapy Perspectives, 35*(2), 219–225. doi:10.1093/mtp/miw025

Knight, A., & Lagasse, B. (2012). Reconnecting to music technology: Looking back and looking forward. *Music Therapy Perspectives, 30*(2), 188–195. doi:10.1093/mtp/30/2/188.

Krout, R., Baker, F., & Muhlberger, R. (2010). Designing, piloting, and evaluating an online collaborative songwriting environment and protocol using Skype telecommunication technology: Perceptions of music therapy students. *Music Therapy Perspectives, 28*(1), 79–855. doi:10.1093/mtp/28.1.79.

Kruger, V. (2007). Music as narrative technology. *Voices: A World Forum for Music Therapy, 7*(2). Retrieved from https://voices.no/index.php/voices/article/view/492/399

Lindeck, J. (2014). Applications of music technology in a children's hospice setting. In W. L. Magee (Ed.), *Music technology in therapeutic and health settings* (pp. 199–213). Jessica Kingsley Publishers.

Magee, W. (2014). *Music technology in therapeutic and health settings.* Jessica Kingsley Publishers.

Magee, W., Bertolami, M., Kubicek, L., Lajoie, M., Martino, L., Sankowski, A., Townsend, J., Whitehead–Pleaux, A., & Buras Zigo, J. (2011). Using music technology in music therapy with populations across the lifespan in medical and educational programs *Music & Medicine, 3*(3), 146–153.

Magee, W. & Burland, K. (2008a). An exploratory study of the use of electronic music technologies in clinical music therapy. *Nordic Journal of Music Therapy, 17*(2), 124–141.

Magee, W. & Burland, K. (2008b). Using electronic music technologies in music therapy: Opportunities, limitations, and clinical indicators. *British Journal of Music Therapy, 22*(1), 3–15.

Magee, W. & Stensæth, K. (2016). The future of technology in music therapy: Towards collaborative models of practice. In C. Dileo (Ed.), *Envisioning the future of music therapy* (pp. 148–157). Philadelphia, PA: Arts and Quality of Life Research Center at Temple University. Retrieved August 20, 2021, from http://www.temple.edu/boyer/researchcenter

Magee., W. L. (2014). Indicators and contraindications for using music technology with clinical populations: When to use and when not to use. In W. L. Magee (Ed.), *Music technology in therapeutic and health settings* (pp. 83–107). Jessica Kingsley Publishers.

Partesotti, E., Peñalba, A., & Manzolli, J. (2018) Digital instruments and their uses in music therapy. *Nordic Journal of Music Therapy, 27*(5), 399–418. doi:10.1080/08098131.2018.1490919

Sadovnik, N. (2014). The birth of a therapeutic recording studio: Addressing the needs of the hip-hop generation on an adult inpatient psychiatric unit. In W. Magee (Ed.), *Music technology in therapeutic and health settings* (pp. 247–262). Jessica Kingsley Publishers.

Schreck, B., & Economos, A. (2018). Heartbeat recording and composing in perinatal palliative care and hospice music therapy. *Music & Medicine, 10*(1), 22–25.

Stensæth, K. (2014). (Ed.). *Music, health, technology, and design*. Series from the Centre for Music and Health (Vol. 7). NMH Publications.

Viega, M. (2018). A humanistic understanding of the use of digital technology in therapeutic songwriting. *Music Therapy Perspectives, 36*(2), 152–160. doi:10.1093/mtp/miy014

Walden, M., Elliot, E., Ghrayeb, A., Lovenstein, A., Ramick, A., Adams, G., Fairchild, B., & Schreck, B. (2021). And the beat goes on: Heartbeat recordings through music therapy for parents with children with progressive neurodegenerative illness. *Journal of Palliative Medicine, 24*(7), 1023–1029. doi:10.1089/jpm.2020.0447

Werger, C., Groothuis, M., & Jaschke, A. Music-based therapeutic interventions 1.0 from music therapy to integrated music technology. *Music & Medicine, 12*(2), 73–83.

Weissberg, A. (2014). GarageBand as Digital Co-Facilitator: Creating and capturing moments with adults and elderly people with chronic health conditions. In W. L. Magee (Ed.), *Music technology in therapeutic and health settings* (pp. 279–294). Jessica Kingsley Publishers.

Index

A

abuse, 53, 85–87, 93–94, 96, 134, 197
accompaniment, 13, 34, 39, 49, 57, 70, 78, 99, 106, 108, 111–12, 114, 149, 151, 208
adaptations, 6, 59, 73, 85, 88, 91, 129, 160, 195
addictions, 52, 55, 64, 90, 124
adolescents, 40, 52–53, 73, 86–87, 92–93, 95–97, 117, 119–20, 128, 130, 134, 185–86, 197–98, 219, 221
adult medical care, 54–55, 92–95, 97, 162, 198–99
affordances, xii–xiv, 5–6, 8–9, 19–23, 27–28, 38–39, 41, 50, 52, 58–59, 101, 138–39, 152–53, 167–68, 195–96
albums, 171, 190–91, 194, 205, 213
applications, xiv, 25, 186, 192, 197, 201, 208–11, 215–18, 220–21
arts media, 162, 169–70, 175, 180, 182
arts modalities, 165, 176–78

B

BMT (bone marrow transplant), 51, 55, 64
brainstorm, 36, 67–68, 110
brainstorming, 31, 36, 50

C

caregivers, 85, 126–27, 131, 133, 160, 162, 198
case examples, xiv–xv, 89, 119, 159–60, 219–20
challenges, 5–9, 11, 16, 23, 27–28, 38, 44, 58–59, 62, 79, 81–82, 100–101, 103, 105, 139–40
chorus, 59, 68, 76–77, 110, 122, 127, 131

client's abilities, 33–34, 47, 82, 84, 145
client's engagement, 6, 8, 84–85, 91, 158, 208–9, 216
client's experience, 10, 15, 63, 71–72
Clinical Decision-Making, 5, 30, 62, 104, 141, 170
Clinical Technology Case, 203–6, 211
collage, 165, 167–73, 175, 179–87
colors, 18, 78–79, 141, 145–46, 157–58
communication, 14–15, 26, 89, 100, 138, 159, 166, 169, 171, 173, 210, 217, 219, 221
Compositional Methods, use of technology in, 72, 203, 205, 207, 209, 211, 213, 215, 217, 219, 221, 223, 225
compositional method-variations, xv, 4–6, 8–9, 12–13, 20, 74, 140, 144, 165, 167–68, 183, 201–3, 215–19, 222
composition process, 13, 89, 123, 125, 129–30, 142, 151, 159–60, 170, 180, 201, 203, 208–10, 219, 221–22
computer technology, 177–78, 220
creating hip-hop songs, 89, 97, 162
creative process, 25, 85, 125–26, 132, 139, 142, 151, 162, 168, 181–82, 186
culture, xiv, 9–10, 12, 73, 196

D

deaf clients, 89, 97
deep listening, 14–15
dementia, 27, 51–53, 55–56, 126, 128–29, 131, 133–35, 139, 198
design, xiii–xv, 4–5, 8, 13, 20, 91, 192, 195–96, 222, 226

devices, 13, 26, 109, 202, 204, 208–11, 214–15, 217
drugs and alcohol, 120–23
drum machine, 121, 203–4, 221
Duchenne Muscular Dystrophy (DMD), 125–26

E

eating disorders, 50, 55–56, 87, 97, 106, 129, 136, 193, 199
emotions, 28–29, 43–44, 47, 73, 75, 77–78, 80–82, 86–87, 142–43, 152, 181, 183, 189, 191, 194
empowerment, 11–12, 50, 69, 103–4, 106, 126, 132
engagement, 80, 83, 88, 91, 108, 110, 112, 114, 123, 125, 128–29, 131, 192, 197, 219
experience, unfamiliar, 62, 100, 102, 112

F

family, 9, 12, 49, 75, 78–79, 90, 186, 206–8, 213–14, 221
family caregivers, 93, 126, 133–34
flexibility, 6, 16, 25, 50–51, 152, 172
formats, 88, 169, 177, 187, 191, 202, 204–6, 213–15
frustration, 21, 37, 58, 69, 138, 147, 171, 181

G

GarageBand, 145, 204, 207, 211, 220, 226
gender, 9–10, 12
genres, 59, 67–68, 70, 101–2, 111, 117, 120, 124, 203–4
group experience, 100, 102–3, 107
group song, 31, 99, 110, 129
group songwriting process, 99, 101, 105–9, 111, 118, 126–27

H

harmony, 25, 27, 31, 35, 47, 127, 131, 137, 140, 146
hearing, 16, 41, 50, 63, 71, 73–74, 115, 118, 124, 151, 159
https, 55–56, 96–97, 134–36, 162, 223–25

I

identity, 9–10, 12, 73, 82, 91, 117, 166, 168–69, 186, 193, 215
instrumental composition, 4, 137, 139–43, 145–47, 149, 151–53, 155, 157–61, 163, 211
instrumentation, 11, 59, 68, 70, 79, 101–2, 111, 131, 137, 159, 176–77, 202, 217
instruments, 4, 12–13, 59, 66, 68–70, 73, 77–79, 84, 109, 111–14, 137–38, 140–41, 143–46, 151–52, 159
 virtual, 211
intent, 14, 21, 36, 39, 140, 146, 148–51, 179
interactions, 7, 14–15, 19, 21–22, 142, 207
intersectionality, xiv, 9–10, 41, 117
Introduction to music therapy practice, 54–55, 93–95, 135, 191, 199, 224
iPad, 211, 214, 220

L

language, 9, 27, 41, 100, 137–41, 143, 151–52, 161
laptop, 66, 109, 202, 204, 206–7, 214
listening, 14, 16, 31–32, 84, 102–3, 105, 111–12, 137, 144, 149, 191, 193, 195, 224
loss, 43, 77, 79–80, 85, 131, 152, 169
lyrics, 28–29, 32, 34–36, 49–50, 57, 59–64, 66–70, 74, 76–77, 79–80,

101–2, 108–11, 120–21, 124–27, 203–4
lyrics and music, 60, 63, 66, 71, 89–90, 105, 115, 117, 126
lyric sheets, 34–35, 44

M

melody, 25, 27–28, 47, 50, 70, 73–74, 78, 81, 99, 110–11, 114, 116, 118, 131, 156–57
melody lines, 78, 116
mental health, 53, 55, 92–97, 128, 130, 133–36, 162, 195, 197, 199, 224
message, 59–61, 63, 68, 81, 103, 114, 121, 127
movement, 38, 62, 158–59, 210–11
musical autobiography, 196–97
musical choices, 71, 76–77, 84, 89, 114, 127, 142, 147
musical elements, 11, 35–36, 40, 62, 70, 80–81, 84, 113–14, 125, 146, 205
musical instrument digital interface (MIDI), 217
musical support, live, 177–78
music collage experience, 166–72, 174–76, 179–87, 191–92, 194–95
music preferences, 41, 59, 65, 73, 92, 108–9, 117
music technology, xv, 218, 221–26
Myers-Coffman, 130–31, 135–36

N

names, 17–20, 45, 140, 157, 215
NICU (Neonatal Intensive Care Unit), 52, 55, 89, 94
notation, 57, 137, 145, 147, 149, 159
notational system, 138, 141, 143–44, 146, 148, 152, 156–59

O

older adults, 41, 47, 52, 54, 73–74, 118, 128, 151–52, 155–56, 186–87
Orientations, xiv, 5–6, 30, 32, 62, 74, 104, 128, 141, 170
original song, 18, 25–29, 32, 35–36, 46, 48–49, 51, 57, 76, 79, 90, 99, 105, 120, 213
outcome orientation, 5–6, 30, 62, 104, 141, 152, 170, 186

P

palliative care, 89, 94, 96, 134, 197, 199, 221, 224, 226
pediatric care, 54–55, 93, 95–96, 162, 198–99
performance, 35, 50, 107, 137, 176–79, 218
planning, 21, 26, 33, 57–58, 76, 80, 90–91, 107–8, 119, 123, 151, 153, 155, 174, 176
playing, 69, 71, 108, 112, 115, 147, 149, 152, 157, 160, 175–77, 180, 193, 195, 209
prerequisites, 23, 25, 57, 99, 138, 166
problem-solving, 7, 26, 28–29, 46, 60, 143

R

relationships, xv, 7, 12, 30, 52, 70, 86, 106–7, 127, 131–32, 165–66, 169, 173, 186, 190
rhythmic structures, 28, 32, 35
rhythms, 11, 59, 62, 66–67, 101, 109–11, 117, 121, 131, 137, 140, 146, 156, 203–5
risks, 10, 21, 23, 26, 58, 60, 100, 103, 138–39, 156, 166–67
Risks and Contraindications, 26, 58, 100, 138, 166

S

safety, 9, 11, 40–41, 61, 73, 85–86, 103, 117, 160, 167, 173
score, 137, 141–42, 145, 147, 150–52, 159
self-awareness, 140, 168, 192
self-expression, 10, 20, 29, 60, 88, 102, 158–59, 168, 192
sing, 18–19, 35, 46, 62, 67–72, 78, 81, 83–84, 110–12, 114–15, 118, 124–25, 176
social skills, 6, 17, 20, 29–30, 92, 142, 166–67, 170–71
song communication, 7–8, 39
song composition, 67–68, 70, 94, 104, 129–30, 133, 135, 213, 220
song content, 31, 48
song lyrics, 59, 66, 68, 83–86, 89, 99, 106, 116, 124, 127, 129, 132, 209
song parody, 47–48
song transformation, 7, 17–20, 25–33, 35, 37, 39–45, 47–55
song transformation experience, 26–33, 35, 41
song transformation method-variation, 35, 49, 51–53
songwriting methods, 90
stories, songscaped life, 193
structuring, 20, 26–27, 47, 87, 128–30, 152, 166, 170

T

time, 30–31, 43–44, 46–47, 68–69, 75–77, 113, 115, 125–26, 139–40, 152, 174, 179, 184, 186, 192–96
tonality, 28, 34, 59, 68, 101, 111
tone chime, 156–57
transformation process, 26, 34, 37–40, 45
transformed song, 25–26, 28–29, 31, 36–39, 46
transitions, 8, 51, 84–85, 87–88, 137, 172, 211
trauma, 10, 12, 53, 80, 85, 87, 94, 129–30, 160, 167, 194, 221
trauma-informed practice, xiv, 10–11
traumatic brain injury (TBI), 84, 88, 92, 96–97, 219, 223
trust, 11–12, 16, 61, 103, 126, 185, 193–94

U

Use of songwriting, 86–87, 128–30

V

voices, 93–94, 96–97, 136–37, 162, 202, 204–5, 207–8, 223–25